SPIRITS HOVERING
OVER THE ASHES

SUNY SERIES IN POSTMODERN CULTURE
JOSEPH NATOLI, EDITOR

SPIRITS HOVERING OVER THE ASHES

Legacies of Postmodern Theory

H. L. Hix

State University of New York Press

Published by
State University of New York Press, Albany

For information, address State University of New York
Press, State University Plaza, Albany, N.Y., 12246

Production by E. Moore
Marketing by Theresa Abad Swierzowski

Library of Congress Cataloging-in-Publication Data

Hix, H. L.
    Spirits hovering over the ashes : legacies of postmodern theory /
H.L. Hix.
        p.   cm. — (SUNY series in postmodern culture)
    Includes bibliographical references.
    ISBN 0-7914-2515-0 (hardcover : alk. paper). — ISBN 0-7914-2516-9
(pbk. : alk. paper)
    1. Postmodernism. 2. Virtue. I. Title. II. Series.
B831.2.H58 1995
149—dc20   94-30816
                                                                      CIP

10 9 8 7 6 5 4 3 2 1

The earlier culture will become a heap of rubble and finally a heap of ashes, but spirits will hover over the ashes.

—Ludwig Wittgenstein, Culture and Value

Contents

Acknowledgments

An earlier version of "Postmodern Grief" was published in *Philosophy and Literature*. An earlier version of the section on Baudrillard was published as "The Nostalgia of Postmodernism" in *Harvard Review*.

Earlier versions of "Postmodern Aporesis" and "Postmodern Love" were published in *Harvard Review*.

An earlier version of part of "Postmodern Freedom" was presented at the Northwest Conference on Philosophy on 9 November 1990, and I am indebted to Michael Bybee for his comments. Another part was published in *Harvard Review*.

An earlier version of "Postmodern Beauty" was presented at the American Society for Aesthetics Western Division Meeting on 3 April 1991, and I am indebted to John Heintz for his generous response and useful comments.

An earlier version of "Postmodern Obscenity" was presented at the Central States Philosophical Association Meeting on 16 October 1993, and I am indebted to David Fairchild for his perspicacious comments.

An earlier version of "Postmodern Censorship" was published as a review in the *New Letters Book Reviewer*.

"Postmodern Color" grew out of an undergraduate seminar on color I offered at the Kansas City Art Institute in the fall of 1993, and it incorporates some of what the students taught me in that class.

Earlier versions of parts of "Postmodern Virtue" were presented at Harvard University on 15 October 1992 and at the University of Nebraska at Kearney on 1 October 1993, and I am indebted to the audience members for many useful responses.

An earlier version of portions of "Postmodern Postscript(s)" was published in *The Iowa Review*.

I am grateful to many people for various forms of support during the writing of this book, notably David Daniel, Lynne McFall,

Rush Rankin, and Paul Woodruff. I thank Joseph Natoli for including this in his series, and Carola Sautter for the capable editorship that metamorphosed it from manuscript to book. Three readers for SUNY Press offered many valuable criticisms and suggestions. Gene Fendt merits special gratitude for giving the entire manuscript a thorough lashing, from which it emerged humbler but wiser.

To no one does this book owe more, though, than to two particular spirits: since before it began, Stratis Haviaras has hovered over the book, and Sheila Pedigo over its author.

1 Postmodern Preface(s)

Can this cockpit hold
The vasty fields of France?
—Shakespeare, Henry V

Nothing is as complicated as we make it, or as simple as we wish it were. Postmodern theorists complicate everything, but nothing more than prefaces. Not that prefaces were ever simple for anyone. Wittgenstein prefaced postmodern theory, and his words in epigraph and title preface this book, but he himself was plagued by the preface. Its complications take the form of torment in *On Certainty*: "It is so difficult to find the beginning. Or, better: it is difficult to begin at the beginning. And not try to go further back" (1972:62e). Those complications become prophecy in this preface to a preface that finds the beginning of a book it did not begin: "The danger in a long foreword is that the spirit of a book has to be evident in the book itself and cannot be described. . . . Even the foreword is written just for those who understand the book" (1980:7e).

Still, for postmoderns the complications lead to histrionics, as exemplified by Derrida when in the preface to *Dissemination* he finds himself in the labyrinth and out of string. "Here is what I wrote, then read, and what I am writing that you are going to read. After which you will again be able to take possession of this preface which in sum you have not yet begun to read, even though, once having read it, you will already have anticipated everything that follows and thus you might just as well dispense with reading the rest" (1981:7). Of course Derrida no more wants you to stop reading than the Cretan liar wants you to stop believing him. Derrida's words are not advice, but an announcement that he finds (and helps to make) the preface both "essential and ludicrous."

Other postmodern theorists regard the preface similarly. Foucault wishes he could be "freed from the obligation to begin" (1972:215), and when he does begin, purports to be preparing only to lose himself, "to have no face" (17). Baudrillard considers writing a preface as untimely and disastrous as Orpheus's looking back at Eurydice: "One must pretend that the work preexisted to itself and forebode its own end from the very beginning. This may be an ill omen" (1988:9). Gayatri Spivak purports to be telling the truth when in a preface she asserts that "the preface harbors a lie" (x). Louis Mackey fulfills his authorial responsibility by pointing out in a preface that a preface is an "irresponsible sanctuary" (xv). Barthes, unwittingly foreshadowing his later proclamation of the "death of the author," finds himself, in the preface to *Critical Essays*, "still as death" (1972:xi). Indeed, for the postmoderns prefaces exude the redolence of remains: "the law of the Preface," John Tagg says, "closes the text of the book as that which has been written, remains written, yet remains to be written" (2).

In order not to be deterred by the prefatory dilemmas to which these and other postmodern theorists allude, I will treat the preface as neither more nor less paradoxical than any other writing. The preface may be an about-face, but merely showing a second Janus face to others does not change the impossibility of facing oneself. The peculiarities of the preface do not *add to* the general paradox that "one has only learnt to get the better of words / For the thing one no longer has to say" (Eliot 1970:188), any more than borrowing from a friend after the credit union says no adds to a person's bankruptcy. Certainly prefaces are no more difficult than any other writing. In writing, as in love, starting is not the most difficult part: any awareness of the need to begin could occur only after one has already begun. The greater difficulty lies in transforming a beginning into the beginning of something valuable. A preface is a promise, and the act of promising is troubling not because *making* promises is hard, but because *keeping* them is hard. The prologues are always already over, and it is now, as it always has been, time to choose.

Although I will try to refuse the difficulties of postmodern prefaces, I will not ignore them. In fact, I think the problem of the preface exposes the spatiotemporal problematic within which postmodern theory occurs. The problem of the preface is a temporal problem, in which what is written after is read before, and it is a spatial problem, in which the preface belongs neither inside nor outside the text. To pursue the Derridean example, prefaces disseminate time: "From the viewpoint of the fore-word, which recreates an intention-to-say after the fact, the text exists as something written—a past—which, under the false appearance of a present, a hidden omnipotent author (in full mastery of his product) is presenting to the reader as his future" (1981:7). They also disseminate space: a preface is a residue "exterior to the development of the content it announces" (9).

Such spatiotemporal problems undercut the preface as the site of definition: if the prefatory definition could succeed, the rest of the book would be superfluous; and if the prefatory definition could not succeed, it would itself be superfluous. Thus I will not here try to answer the obligatory "what is postmodernism?", for several reasons. For one thing, I doubt that the word *postmodern* denotes some entity that precedes it. Certainly, it does not pick out a time period, the one following the modern period: "neither modernity nor so-called postmodernity," Lyotard says, "can be identified and defined as clearly circumscribed historical entities, of which the latter would always come 'after' the former" (1991:25). *Postmodern* does not pick out a time period, or anything else for that matter. "No doubt there 'is' no such 'thing' as postmodernism," says Brian McHale. Like 'the Renaissance,' 'American literature,' and 'Shakespeare,' postmodernism "exists discursively, in the discourses we produce *about* it and *using* it" (1).

Another reason I will not define *postmodern* is my doubt that the term is used in ways consistent enough to be amenable to definition. Like Wittgenstein's games, the many uses of *postmodern* may have a number of "family resemblances," but none of those resemblances are shared by all the uses. My own uses in the chapters that follow will aim less for consistency than for flexibility, in order to err on the side of expansiveness rather than exclusion. I will take the wide range of family resemblances as permission to treat Barthes and Lévi-Strauss alongside Deleuze and Baudrillard, for instance, in spite of their differences from each other.

Finally, to answer the question "what is postmodernism?" at all accepts the whole metaphysics of essence and linguistics of reference against which postmodern theories are directed, just as answering either yes or no to the question "do you still beat your wife?" implies guilt. This preface will purport neither to solve the problems of the postmodern preface, nor simply to reenact them by replaying the following chapters liminally and after the fact, but instead to take postmodern prefatory problems as a heuristic revealing that the transition from modernism to postmodernism was/is marked by a shift in emphasis from the temporal to the spatial. Here, as in the chapters that follow, I am less interested in accurately describing an allegedly coherent phenomenon or faithfully interpreting an allegedly related set of documents than I am in extorting from them ways of thinking I can live with. Instead, then, of reiterating as a preface what the other chapters (will) have already iterated, I will follow in/as my preface two texts that themselves serve already as prefaces to postmodernism.

First, Saussure. "The linguist who wishes to understand a state must discard all knowledge of everything that produced it and ignore diachrony. He can enter the mind of speakers only by completely suppressing the past. The intervention of history can only falsify his judgment" (81). This denigration of history is one of the founding gestures of postmodernism, asserting as it does that meaning is generated across space rather than time. Compare Saussure's view to the faith in history espoused by moderns like Eliot and Santayana.

Eliot thinks meaning is constituted by diachrony. The meaning of great poems arises because they manage to internalize the history of great poems, indeed "the whole of the literature of Europe from Homer" (1975:38). Diachrony governs the act of creation, since the poet must "develop or procure the consciousness of the past" (40), and also governs the reception of the work, which can only be valued by setting the artist, "for contrast and comparison, among the dead" (38), and by judging the artist according to "the standards of the past" (39). The great poem means by acting across time: "what happens when a new work of art is created is something that happens simultaneously to all the works of art which preceded it" (38). Even the present itself is historically constituted: in a work of art the present is conscious not of itself but of the past.

Santayana is best known for the faith in diachrony encapsulated in his apothegm that ignorance of history condemns one to repeat it. Like Eliot, Santayana privileges diachrony over synchrony. Indeed, hardly more than his emphasis on epistemology rather than aesthetics separates Santayana's view from Eliot's. For Santayana, belief rather than poetry is the end, but history (as *memory* rather than *tradition*) is still the means: "mind and memory," he writes, as if condemned to repeat Augustine's *Confessions*, "are indeed names for almost the same thing" (425).

Unlike the preface to a book, which presages the writing it postdates, Saussure's preface to postmodernism antedates the modernist ideas it supersedes. That Saussure could produce a view so nearly opposite the later views of Eliot and Santayana shows the extent to which modernism was a deformation of space and time. Spatially, Plato's cave, the womb from which, by maieusis, one escapes to enlightenment, and to which one returns out of obligation to enlighten others, becomes Kafka's burrow, the tomb into which one escapes from the unbearable light and noise of the truth. Dante's inferno, through which he passes on the way to paradise, is transmuted into Eliot's wasteland, "a brown land" where there are only "mountains of rock without water," from which "the nymphs are departed," but from which for us there is no escape. Sophocles' exile, to which Oedipus voluntarily accedes in order to salvage nobility from his defeat by Fate, becomes Marx's alienation, which separates us against our will not only from our home, but also from our work, our potential, our humanity, and ourselves.

Temporally, the future of the gospels, toward which we march and in which the sheep and the goats will be separated by the zoology of divine truth, becomes the future of "The Second Coming," toward which we slouch and in which the "lion body and the head of a man" will be joined by a teratology of nightmare. The temporal field of Descartes, in which the subject's self-presence cannot be severed, even by "the most extravagant suppositions" (101), becomes the temporal torus of the *Tractatus*, exclusion from which erases both death (6.4311) and the subject (5.631-32) from the world. The unified time of Augustine, held together by divine logos, revelation of which holds the promise of peace, devolves into the fragmented time of Freud, pieced together by the analyst into a mythos, peace from which is offered at the price of revelation.

Modernism's deformation of space and time prepares for postmodernism's privileging of space over time. Postmodernism does not only become ahistorical, as William E. Grim suggests by invoking Schiller's "dichotomy between the sentimental and the naive: the former being art that is conscious of its antecedents, the latter being art that is unaware of its past" (154), but becomes ahistorical in a certain way—namely, by trading time for space. Saussure's insight that structure rather than succession signifies was made possible by modernism's malleation of space and time, and in its own prescience provided a preface to postmodernism, paving the way for all the postmodern markers. From Foucault's archaeology, which to find out about the history of a site must first make the site into a grid, to Baudrillard's simulation, which eliminates representation by eliminating spatial order, from Lacan's *objet petit a*, which is separated from itself by an unbridgeable gap, to Derrida's parergon, which is both inside and outside the work, all are constituted by synchrony in preference to diachrony.

The privileging of space over time is neither without cause nor without consequence. Here I cite as a second preface to postmodernism a passage from Nietzsche. "The time has come," he writes in *The Will to Power*, "when we have to pay for having been Christians for two thousand years: we are losing the center of gravity by virtue of which we lived; we are lost for a while. Abruptly we plunge into the opposite valuations, with all the energy that such an extreme overvaluation of man has generated in man. Now everything is false through and through, mere 'words'" (1968b:20).

The obsolescence of Christianity meant the obsolescence of diachrony. In Christianity, time is divine and linear: it began when God told it to, and will end when God chooses. That makes time God's time, but it also makes time humanity's time, because it began when we (the world) began, and will end when we end. In the time of Christianity, events always move forward, and they always mean, because they are means to a divine end. The future is inexorable, and in it all meaning will be revealed. "For now we see through a glass, darkly; but then face to face: now I know in part; but then shall I know even as also I am known." At the death of God, though, diachrony becomes synchrony. If St. Paul is concerned about time, Nietzsche's madman is concerned about space: "What were we doing when we unchained this earth from its sun? Whither is it moving now? Whither are we moving? Away from all suns? Are we not plunging continually? Backward, sideward, forward, in all directions? Is there still any up or down? Are we not straying as through an infinite nothing? Do we not feel the breath of empty space? Has it not become colder?" (1974:181).

Christianity oriented us in time, by providing temporal ideals like hope and by grounding identity in temporal capacities like memory. It offered a temporal mechanism, confession / absolution, for moral orientation. Postmodern theory has been left the task of providing equivalent spatial ideals, capacities, and mechanisms to orient us after the loss of Christianity.

The word *postmodernism* itself indicates that the substitution of synchrony for diachrony is a form of apocalypticism. The problem is not that the end is near, but that the end is already past. Postmodernism is chiliastic. "Every few thousand years," Bob Perelman says, "the past has got to go" (69). Words become "mere" words when diachrony disappears, as the modernist Eliot revealed when his attempt to say that "the end and the beginning were always there" and "all is always now" resulted in a conclusion not about time per se, but about meaning: "Words strain, / Crack and sometimes break, under the burden" (1970:180). Elimination of diachrony in favor of synchrony eliminates the *archē*, that equivalence of temporal and ontological priority, and by leaving the postmoderns, unlike the pre-Socratics, without an object, imposes the problem of the preface. Depriving meanings of their beginnings also deprives beginnings of their meanings. Electrons may have survived the loss of temporal sequence, but meaning has not. As Kant had to catch up with Newton, to find (or concoct) the simple and inviolable laws governing human thought and activity, so postmodern theory is trying to catch up with Einstein and Heisenberg, to find out how to talk and to live when space and time are relative and location indeterminate.

Postmodern theorists' discomfort with prefaces arises in part from their having rightly discerned that, insofar as a preface is a summary or recapitulation of the content of the text it precedes, either the preface or the text must be superfluous. If the preface fails to reproduce the text's content, it is unnecessary; if it succeeds, the text is unnecessary. Having assimilated at least that much of the wisdom of the postmoderns, I have not tried to reiterate in this preface the content of the chapters that follow. I have no such reservations, though, about the ability of prefaces to summarize purpose, and conclude this preface with as forthright a statement of purpose as I know how to make, or believe writing can convey.

My objective in writing and publishing this book is neither to advocate *postmodernism* (as if it were a unified entity susceptible to advocacy, or the sort of phenomenon that my support would advance) nor to deride it (which would be about as effective as complaining about the weather), but instead to explore it as part of a continuing attempt to find out how to live now, not as an exile of the past but as a citizen of the present and a progenitor of the future. It may be that, as David Lehman says, "The Twentieth Century is the name of a train that no longer runs," but the twentieth century got us where we are, and we cannot afford to stay. Postmodern theory attempts to describe our location, and I want in my exploration of it neither to oversimplify ideas that are richly layered, nor to over-complicate ideas that are often deliberately obfuscated; to treat the theorists neither as biblical prophets whose words intimidate kings by their possession of the authority of divinity and the weight of the future, nor as Kafka's couriers who "hurry about the world, shouting to each other—since there are no kings—messages that have become meaningless" (1946:185). Like the narrator of J. M. Coetzee's *Age of Iron*, "I am trying to keep a soul alive in times not hospitable to the soul" (1990:130). My aim is to discover whether and how it is possible for an individual citizen of our time to read in the conclusion of this millennium instruction in how to write a better preface for the next.

2 Postmodern Grief

Thou seest we are not all alone unhappy:
This wide and universal theatre
Presents more woeful pageants than the scene
Wherein we play in.
                    —*Shakespeare,* As You Like It

Thought is a form of grief. Plato knew this when he described learning as recollection from previous lives, Kant when in the first *Critique* he reluctantly acknowledged that desperation alone grounds our most cherished knowledge claims, Freud when he identified intellectual inquiry as one of the forms of sublimated sexuality, and Wittgenstein when his youthful solution to all the problems of philosophy culminated in an ominously Job-like silence. "The death everywhere is no trouble," Jack Gilbert says, "once you see it as nature, landscape, or botany" (53). Thought may lament the loss of the mother (as in Freud), the father (as in Plato), or the world (as in Hegel). It may lament the loss of innocence (as in Nietzsche), knowledge (as in Kant), or hope (as in Camus). Thought may lament the immanent loss of oneself; perhaps any lament is a lament for the immanent loss of oneself. But think we do, and lament we must, because lose we will.

   Thought is a form of grief, and postmodern thought is no exception. We postmoderns, and we are all postmoderns, have much to lament. The century at whose bang (or whimper) we will preside has been the scene of holocaust, famine, two world wars, the dropping of the atomic bomb, terrorism, unprecedented destruction of natural resources, and the mass destruction of whole segments of society by drugs: more of what Auden calls "the facts of filth and violence / that we're too dumb to prevent" (1976:658) than in any previous century. My concern here, though, is with the dramatic change in communications technology that, although a less obvious occasion for grief, is a more immediate occasion for what is usually called postmodern thought.

The information age, cyberspace, the global village, the postmodern condition: call it what you will. The future will be, if the present has not become already, binary, brought to us by optical fiber and silicon, scrolling out of facsimile machines and appearing on video terminals. Out of the sea we came, and into a blue-green brine of computer monitors we are returning. No one denies that technological changes are now more rapid and more pervasive than ever before: the origins of writing and print were separated by five thousand years of human culture; television and the pc-editable hand-held video camera by less than fifty. We have less readily acknowledged, though, what postmodern theory has insisted on: when technology transforms our homes and workplaces, we too are transformed.

The transformation itself is often transparent, because of what O. B. Hardison calls the "Great Wall Syndrome." The presence of the Great Wall was, according to Hardison, virtually unnoticed until it ceased to perform its original function. Not until it could no longer be viewed as "something that keeps somebody out" (84), not in other words until it ceased to be useful, did it confront its percipients as a wonder of the world. As Hardison goes on to point out, though, the transparence of the transformation wrought on us by our technology does not diminish its pervasiveness. Even a technology as useful and transparent as clocks has irreversibly altered us. "By permitting precise control of time, clocks also changed the nature of work, turning the day into standard and repeatable segments and permitting wages to be related to hours of work. Clocks therefore contributed mightily to making human behavior more 'like' the behavior of machines. This is a significant point because the introduction of machines that are like people into society is usually considered a one-way street. It is not" (295). When we make machines like ourselves, they make us like themselves.

That much of postmodernism, though, should not have surprised us. As long ago as 1931 to 1932, the Russian neuropsychologist A. R. Luria conducted a study among illiterate and newly literate collective farm workers in central Asia to show "that the structure of cognitive activity does not remain static during different stages of historical development and that the most important forms of cognitive processes—perception, generalization, deduc-

tion, reasoning, imagination, and analysis of one's own inner life—
vary as the conditions of social life change" (1976:161). In other
words, changes in social practice not only change our ideas, but
"radically affect the structure of cognitive processes." Luria studied
subjects experiencing changes in literacy because no other type of
social change affects cognitive processes as directly or as radically as
changes in the transmission, acquisition, storing, and exchange of
cognitive materials. Postmodern thought is crucial because never
before have the modes of processing cognitive materials changed
so much or so rapidly.

The advent of electronic media, including such devices as telephones, radios, fax machines, computers, modems, televisions, pho-
tocopiers, and laser disc players is bringing about the most radical
change in the mode of manipulation of cognitive materials in human
history. And it is producing, whether we like it or not, changes in the
structure of our cognitive processes. But only in its magnitude is
the change without precedent.

Our social change resembles the change experienced by the
ancient Greeks for a period of several centuries after they derived
their alphabet from that of the Phoenicians ca. 750-700 B.C. The significance of the change from an oral to a written culture in Greece
has been well documented by Eric A. Havelock in his *Preface to
Plato*. Havelock argues that Plato's ideas would not have been possible without the invention of writing, and that Plato's ideas are
very largely a response to the transition from speech to writing as the
dominant discursive mode. Even though the technology of writing,
on Havelock's view, is for Plato both explanans and explanandum,
Plato's work displays a strong element of resistance to writing.
Nowhere is that element of resistance more explicit than near the
end of the *Phaedrus*, where Socrates tells the myth of Theuth's presentation of writing (along with other *technai* he had invented, like
geometry and astronomy) to the Egyptian king Thamus. Theuth
brags that writing "will make the people of Egypt wiser and improve
their memories," but Thamus replies that the people "will cease to
exercise memory because they rely on that which is written, calling
things to remembrance no longer from within themselves, but by
means of external marks." To Thamus, "it is no true wisdom that
you offer your disciples, but only its semblance" (Plato 520-21).
Socrates contends that writing is ultimately damaging rather than
edifying, because it externalizes what should be internal, and substitutes appearance for reality.

From our current coign, Socrates' conclusion that writing primarily damages appears to be wrong. But he was right to prophesy that writing would change noesis dramatically and irreversibly. And he was right to grieve: like any prophet, when he descried the future, he also decried it. Postmodern theorists, too, prophesy, this time that electronic communication technologies are changing contemporary noesis as irreversibly as writing changed Greek noesis. Like Socrates', their pronouncements about the future include paeans in praise of the past. Like Socrates, in other words, they are grieving over the loss of a culture.

The five stages of grief identified by Elisabeth Kübler-Ross in her popular book *On Death and Dying* help to reveal as grief ideas we might otherwise mistake for disinterested reflection.

Denial

Kübler-Ross's first stage of grief is denial and isolation. She reports that among the patients she interviewed, "most reacted to the awareness of [their] terminal illness at first with the statement, 'No, not me, it cannot be true'" (38). She attributes this reaction to our inability to confront death continually; we can "consider the possibility of [our] own death [only] for a little while" (39). Denial is a healthy reaction, because it "functions as a buffer" and gives the patient time to "mobilize other, less radical defenses." Although denial is usually temporary, patients may revert to it in times of unusual stress.

Jacques Derrida's writings exemplify the strategy of denial, especially "Plato's Pharmacy," which attends to the same Theuth and Thamus myth from the *Phaedrus* that so succinctly summarizes Socrates' analogical grief. In "Plato's Pharmacy" Derrida argues for the now famous claim that "there is nothing outside the text" (1981:35-36). Socrates asserts an intimate connection between speech and truth, and contends that writing is a disruption of that connection; Derrida agrees that writing is disruptive, but suggests that there is only writing and disruption, not speech and truth.

As his title (for all his resistance to titles) indicates, the key to Derrida's criticism is the Greek word *pharmakon*, to which "Socrates compares the written texts Phaedrus has brought along," and which can mean several things, among them medicine and poison. "This *pharmakon*, this 'medicine,' this philter, which acts as both remedy and poison, already introduces itself into the body of the discourse with all its ambivalence" (70). The *Phaedrus* was for years read as "a badly composed dialogue" (66), aimless and disconnected, but Derrida argues that the *Phaedrus* is strictly ordered: the uses of *pharmakon* follow a "regular, ordered polysemy" (71). "The spontaneity, freedom, and fantasy attributed to Plato in his legend of Theuth were actually supervised and limited by rigorous necessities. The organization of the myth conforms to powerful constraints" (85). The constraints, Derrida says, are not those of speech, as Socrates would have it, but those of writing.

"Plato thinks of writing," according to Derrida, "and tries to comprehend it, to dominate it, on the basis of opposition as such": contrary values like good / evil and essence / appearance must precede and exceed writing (103). Writing copies speech, but its mimesis is no more successful than painting's imitation of material objects. "Writing is considered a consolation, a compensation, a remedy for sickly speech" (115), a view that "will not fail to re-edit itself at least in Rousseau, and then in Saussure" (158). But Derrida contends instead that writing, "far from being governed by these oppositions, opens up their very possibility without letting itself be comprehended by them." In other words, writing structures these oppositions rather than being structured by them. Writing makes speech possible, instead of being made possible by it.

That there is nothing outside the text means for Derrida that nothing precedes or exceeds writing. Nothing escapes the written, because there is no outside to which it could escape. "In a word, we do not believe that there exists, in all rigor, a Platonic text, closed upon itself, complete with its inside and outside" (130). Writing wins inevitably: "The play of the other within being must needs be designated 'writing' by Plato in a discourse which would like to think of itself as spoken in essence, in truth, and which nevertheless is written" (163).

"Plato's Pharmacy" exemplifies denial because, like Southern Baptists fighting textbook committees over evolution, it addresses yesterday's problem. It defends writing against the medium that allegedly preceded it, instead of against the media that threaten to supersede it. Derrida's response to the cultural transformation brought on by media technologies is to deny its occurrence. He rightly criticizes Socrates for failing to confront the possibility that the mode of discourse that superseded speech also preceded it, without recognizing that his act of criticizing Socrates' failure repeats that failure. Socrates lived during the transition from logos to grapheme, and insisted on the privilege of the former. Derrida lives during the transition from character to bit, and insists on the privilege of the former. His doing so is an act of denial.

So-called postmodern thinkers are not alone, though, either in addressing the issues raised by electronic media or in grieving over the cultural losses. Two writers more antithetical than Jacques Derrida and Wendell Berry would be hard to find, yet Berry's controversial essay "Why I Am Not Going to Buy a Computer" is in the same stage of denial as Derrida's essay. Berry refuses to buy a computer for a number of reasons, among them that his wife's manual typewriter still works well, that he wishes not to depend on strip-mined coal, that he considers the sales tactics of computer manufacturers deplorable, that a computer would be expensive, and the like. Berry prefers the past ("I do not see anything wrong with it") to the future (information about which "does not impress me"). He considers himself able to refuse any cultural change brought on by computers. His denial is beautifully summarized in the last sentence of his essay, which is also the culmination of a list of "standards for technological innovation in my own work" (171). The only technological change he will accept is a change that is no change, one that does not "replace or disrupt anything good that already exists, and this includes family and community relationships" (172). Berry's response to the postmodern is to insist of the modern that "It ain't broke."

Anger

Anger inevitably follows denial in the grief process, according to Kübler-Ross. When one can no longer deny one is dying, "the logical next question becomes: 'Why me?,'" and the result of asking oneself this question is "feelings of anger, rage, envy, and resentment" (50). The anger is "displaced in all directions and projected onto the environment." Anyone or anything may become the target of the patient's frustration: doctors, nurses, family members, the television, hospital conditions, and so on.

Like "Plato's Pharmacy," published in 1972, Umberto Eco's "Towards a Semiological Guerrilla Warfare," published in 1967, was written during the early stages of our growing awareness of the cultural impact of communication technologies (or in the language of this essay, during the early stages of our grief). Although Eco repents of his anger in an essay ("The Multiplication of the Media") written sixteen years later but published in the same volume, the warfare alluded to in the title of "Towards a Semiological Guerrilla Warfare" is the first indication that at this stage he is angry. The target of Eco's anger is "those who . . . control information media" (135).

If Eco's anger resembles the anger of Kübler-Ross's paradigmatic dying patient in being "displaced and projected," it differs from the patient's anger in its justification. The patient cannot explain why he or she is angry at the doctor or family members, but Eco begins his essay with an explanation for why he is angry at those who control media. "Not long ago, if you wanted to seize political power in a country, you had merely to control the army and the police." But no longer. "The day after the fall of Khrushchev, the editors of *Pravda*, *Izvestiia*, the heads of the radio and television were replaced; the army wasn't called out. Today a country belongs to the person who controls communications" (135). According to Eco, the Marxian problem of alienation is different for the control of communications than for control of the means of production, because even if control changed hands, "the situation of subjection would not change" (136). In other words, Eco sees the information media situation as futile. A sense of futility (like that imposed by knowledge of the imminence of one's death) inevitably leads to anger, which is, as Sartre says, "not a hereditary curse or a destiny but simply an inept reaction to a too complicated problem" (33).

Eco describes two common views about the dilemma posed by communications technology. The first, held by "the severest critics of mass culture," and labeled "apocalyptic" by Eco, holds that mass media constitute a "call to narcotic passiveness," and believes that "when the mass media triumph, the human being dies" (136-37). The second, espoused by Marshall McLuhan, holds the optimistic, religious view that "when the mass media triumph, the Gutenbergian human being dies, and a new man is born, accustomed to perceive the world in another way." But Eco's anger will let him be satisfied with neither the resignation implicit in the first view nor the hopefulness implicit in the second; thus his call for war, for "the battle of man against the technological universe of communication" (142).

Eco's call to arms involves only one strategic disclosure: the cultural guerrilla must attack not "where the communication originates, but where it arrives." The addressee of mass communication

can maintain an idiosyncratic code "originating in his social situation, in his previous education, and in the psychological tendencies
of the moment" (141), a code that allows the addressee rather than
the source to control the message received from the signal. Beyond
that, "the methods of [the] cultural guerrilla have to be worked out"
(143). The goal of the strategy is clear enough, though: "I am proposing an action to urge the audience to control the message and its
multiple possibilities of interpretation." Like Marx in response to
industrialism, Eco is angered in response to media technology by
its threat of enforced passivity, and like Marx he calls for activity in
the form of battle against the threat.

Allan Bloom, though hardly a "postmodern," exemplifies the
same stage of grief as Eco. In fact, Bloom's "displacement and projection" more closely resembles that of Kübler-Ross's patient than
does Eco's. Bloom is angry about the shallowness and semiliteracy of
his students, for which he blames, not the entire phenomenon of
media technology and its use, but only rock music. "Nothing," he
says, "is more singular about this generation than its addiction to
music" (68). Rock music taps "the rawest passions" just as Plato
prophetically warned Bloom it would; it is "arousing and cathartic"
and encourages "rebellion against the parental authority that
represses it"; and it disguises selfishness as morality. Bloom has
passed the stage of denial: "the continuing exposure to rock music
[Bloom's synecdoche for media culture] is a reality" (75). But his
hyperbolic claims reveal that he has not passed the stage of anger.
"Nothing noble, sublime, profound, delicate, tasteful or even decent
can find a place in such a tableaux" (74). "It is of historic proportions
that a society's best young and their best energies should be so occupied. People of future civilizations will wonder at this and find it as
incomprehensible as we do the caste-system, witch-burning, harems,
cannibalism and gladiatorial combats" (75). If Bloom is right that
"indignation is the soul's defense" against self-doubt, he could hardly
have revealed his own soul's self-doubt more openly than in the
grief over media culture he deflects as anger onto rock music.

Bargaining

Kübler-Ross describes bargaining as the attempt to enter "into some
sort of an agreement which may postpone the inevitable happen-
ing" (82). It imitates a technique at which children are expert. When

a parent has denied a child's request, the child may pout in its room (denial and isolation, stage one) or throw a tantrum (anger, stage two), but if those two techniques fail, probably will "volunteer to do some tasks around the house, which under normal circumstances we never succeeded in getting them to do, and then tell us, 'If I am very good all week and wash the dishes every evening, then will you let me go?'" That with which one bargains may be well- or ill-defined.

Jean-François Lyotard's *The Postmodern Condition* grieves by bargaining. Like the child's request to its parents, Lyotard's thesis takes the form of an if-then. The child says "if I wash the dishes, my parents will let me go." Lyotard says, "if we will distribute knowledge equitably, power will distribute itself equitably."

One of the ways in which technology has changed us, according to Lyotard, is by replacing "metanarratives," like "the dialectics of Spirit, the hermeneutics of meaning, the emancipation of the rational or working subject, or the creation of wealth" (1984:xxiii), with a "logic of maximum performance" modeled on technology itself. The loss of metanarratives entails a linguistic exteriorization and fragmentation, a separation of knowledge from ourselves, and the logic of maximal performance carries with it "a certain level of terror" because it carries the threat "be operational (that is, commensurable) or disappear" (xxiv). Lyotard's bargain (like Eco's call to arms) is hardly new, even if its use as a response to contemporary technoculture is. If we will give to all humans free access to knowledge, Lyotard says, then we will diminish the threat of terror.

Lyotard begins with the fact of loss. "The status of knowledge is altered as societies enter what is known as the postindustrial age and cultures enter what is known as the postmodern age" (3). This alteration takes a particular form—namely, exteriorization: knowledge is taken outside the knower. Also, this alteration in the status of knowledge has particular results—namely, that "the old principle that the acquisition of knowledge is indissociable from the training (*Bildung*) of minds, or even of individuals, is becoming obsolete," and that knowledge is no longer an end in itself, but has become a commodity to be exchanged (4-5). The first consequence of this loss for Lyotard is political. Modernism conceived of only "two basic representational models for society: either society forms a functional whole, or it is divided in two" (11). Either society is an organic whole, or it is based on class struggle. But postmodernism initiates a third alternative: as knowledge becomes externalized from humans, humans become externalized from the functions of society.

"Functions of regulation . . . are being and will be further withdrawn from administrators and entrusted to machines" (14). Thus access to the information the machines process is for Lyotard the crucial ingredient of power, since only through such access can we have any power. Previously society made humans either one or two; now only such access can keep us from being zero.

Unfortunately, when conjoined with the logic of maximal performance, access to knowledge is governed by economic criteria. "Devices that optimize the performance of the human body for the purpose of producing proof require additional expenditures. No money, no proof—and that means no verification of statements and no truth. The games of scientific language become the games of the rich, in which whoever is wealthiest has the best chance of being right. An equation between wealth, efficiency, and truth is thus established" (44-45). This enforces the obsolescence of "idealist and humanist narratives of legitimation" because "in the discourse of today's financial backers of research, the only credible goal is power" (46). In the absence of idealist and humanist legitimation narratives, and under the influence of the scientific method, which needs dissension in order to progress toward maximal performance, "consensus has become an outmoded and suspect value" (66).

For one who believes, as does Lyotard, that "justice as a value is neither outmoded nor suspect," the postmodern neglect of consensus occasions grief. But it also occasions Lyotard's bargain: if I let consensus go, will you let me keep justice? Lyotard believes the bargain can be achieved by keeping power local, and access to knowledge universal. The localization of power can be attained by making the only appropriate response to the fact of "the heteromorphous nature of language games"; in contrast, terror mistakenly treats language games as "isomorphic" (66). Universal access to knowledge is also "quite simple: give the public free access to the memory and data banks" (67). Like the patient who knows that death always gets its way or the child who knows that the parents can always get their way, Lyotard knows the postmodern world will go its own way. But like the patient who wants to live or the child who wants to go to the movie, Lyotard in his desire to retain justice attempts to strike a bargain. Localized power combined with universal knowledge will produce a postmodernism "that would respect both the desire for justice and the desire for the unknown."

Stanley Cavell exemplifies the strategy of bargaining in his essay "The Fact of Television." He is past denial, since "the sheer fact that television exists" is "at once among the most obvious and the most mysterious facts of contemporary life" (1984:235-36); and he is certainly not angry over that sheer fact. But he is ready to bargain. Cavell focuses on the uniqueness of the "mode of perception" necessitated by the "material basis" of television, distinguishing that mode of perception not only from the mode of perception necessitated by writing but even from that of film; television's mode of perception is "monitoring" (252). For Cavell, the problem, the reason for our fear of television, is that monitoring currently "makes intuitive" the "growing uninhabitability of the world, the irreversible pollution of the earth" (267-68). We displace that intuition onto the monitor itself. Cavell bases his bargain on an aesthetics of self-consciousness for the medium of television. If its formats will more consistently be (and be understood as) "revelations (acknowledgments) of the condition of monitoring" (252), if in other words we will acknowledge how we see, we can conquer "the fear of what we see, and wish to see" (267). Monitoring has characteristics, like blurring the "distinction between the live and the repeat" (253), that increase our anxiety over the "loss of our humanity" threatened by the uninhabitability of the world. But, bargains Cavell, better, more self-conscious monitoring (probing by television "for intelligent connections and for beauty among its events") might help us "do something intelligent" about the cause of anxiety (268).

Depression

Depression, Kübler-Ross says, occurs when the patient can no longer deny the terminal nature of the illness, after the anger has proven fruitless, and after bargaining has failed. She distinguishes between two kinds of depression: *reactive* depression looks backward and deals with the insurmountability of what has already been lost; *preparatory* depression looks forward and deals with the inevitability of what will be lost.

In the second sentence of his "Introduction" to *The Ecstasy of Communication*, Jean Baudrillard gives away his reactive depression when he alludes to the myth of Orpheus and Eurydice. Robert Hass says that "nostalgia locates desire in the past where it suffers no active conflict and can be yearned toward pleasantly" (5); Baudrillard's nostalgia fits that definition more literally than Hass meant it. According to Baudrillard, desire is now located only in our past, because we have confused "desire and its equivalent material-ized in the image," so that "images have become our true sex object" (1988:35). Socrates lamented the jettisoning of memory from the internal to the external: memory makes us full, but writing threatens to empty us. Baudrillard laments the loss of dimension: alienation makes us deep, but the screen and the network make us shallow. The social practices that have (inevitably) grown up around elec-tronic media deprive the world of depth and time, leaving it flat, in possession of only two dimensions instead of the four it once pos-sessed.

In place of desire we have only what Baudrillard calls ecstasy. "Ecstasy is all functions abolished into one dimension, the dimen-sion of communication. All events, all spaces, all memories are abol-ished in the sole dimension of information" (23-24). Everything has become surface, because "the distinction between an interior and an exterior . . . has been blurred," and without an interior there can be no depth. The blurring, in turn, results from "a *double obscenity.* The most intimate operation of your life becomes the potential graz-ing ground of the media," as in "real cops" shows, home video shows, and daytime talk shows; and "the entire universe . . . unfolds unnecessarily on your home screen" (20-21). Desire is the pleasure of manifestation, a four-dimensional state that because it confronts otherness contains depth, but ecstasy is only the pleasure of fasci-nation, which is two-dimensional because it lacks an object.

For Baudrillard "the scene [the four-dimensional locus of action] and the mirror [which reflects the subject] have given way to a screen [a two-dimensional locus] and a network [in which there is no subject, only relations]" (12). As a consequence of that "giving way" we lose several things: "we [can] no longer invest our objects with the same emotions," we no longer act or enact except "as ter-minals of multiple networks" (16), "there is no longer a system of objects" but only one of exchange and use (11), "there is nothing to see" because there is nothing hidden and nothing to hide (30-33), there is no more transcendence because where there are only two dimensions there can be nothing over or beyond (55), and there is no "religious, metaphysical or philosophical definition of being" because they have "given way to an operational definition in terms of the genetic code (DNA) and cerebral organization" (50).

Electronic media and the social practices that have blistered around them have had no more dramatic effect on the structure of cognitive processes, according to Baudrillard, than in their elimination of time and space. Kant removed the "transcendental ideality" of time and space, or took them away, in other words, from things in themselves; but he left intact their "empirical reality," or in other words their necessity as conditions for any possible human experience. Baudrillard, in contrast, thinks that even as conditions of experience time and space no longer exist. "Picturing others and everything which brings you closer to them is futile from the instant that 'communication' can make their presence immediate. Imagining time in its length and complexity is futile from the moment that any project is amenable to its immediate execution" (42). We experience the same lack as the rain forest indigene, brought for the first time to a plain, for whom distant cows can be cognized only as proximate insects, but we experience that lack for a different reason: not because we have never seen a horizon, but because "all the horizons have already been traversed."

Our situation has so altered our cognitive processes that according to Baudrillard we are not even subject to the same illnesses as before. Previously, we suffered from hysteria, in which the mental was projected out onto the body, and paranoia, in which the confrontation with the external world is absolutized, made "rigid and jealous." Now, "with the emergence of an immanent promiscuity and the perpetual interconnection of all information and communication networks," we experience the characteristics of schizophrenia: "a foul promiscuity of all things which beleaguer and penetrate [the patient], meeting with no resistance, and no halo, no aura, not even the aura of his own body protects him" (27). Not "loss of touch with reality, but . . . the absolute proximity to and total instantaneousness with things," makes the schizophrenic unable to "produce the limits of his very being," able only to function as "a pure screen, a pure absorption and resorption surface of the influent networks."

After a book of reactive depression, Baudrillard's conclusion is the first hint of preparatory depression. In it he confronts a future whose character is inevitable. He says society has trapped itself into a state of permanent ecstasy (82): "this electronic encephalization, this miniaturization of circuits and of energy, this transistorization of the environment condemn to futilty, to obsolescence and almost to obscenity, all that which once constituted the stage of our lives" (17). The cancer eating our culture is, on Baudrillard's view, malignant.

Charles Bernstein, too, is depressed about electronic technology, as his "Play It Again, Pac-Man" reveals. He identifies a number of reasons for preparatory depression over computers and related phenomena like video games. For instance, they "create an artificial economy of scarcity," or in other words a goal-oriented atmosphere of accumulation, but they do so "in a medium characterized by plenitude," which "stigmatizes them as wastes of time, purposeless, idle" (130-31). The computer "infantilizes our relation to the external" by presenting its contents on command, like "the infant's world as described by Piaget, where objects seem to disappear when you turn your back on them or close your eyes" (135). Bernstein agrees with Baudrillard that the screen negates time and space, and that the result is simulation: "the risks [in a video game] are simulated, the mastery imaginary; only the compulsiveness is real" (139). But his depression is grounded finally in something that Bernstein sees as more basic: namely, that computers reveal our own weakness and illness. "The Alien who keeps coming at us in so many of these [video] games is ourselves"; "what we are fighting is the projection of our sense of inferiority before our own creation" (141). Computers are depressing, Bernstein implies, because they remind us who we are.

Acceptance

Patients who have enough time and receive appropriate support reach at last a stage during which they are "neither depressed nor angry" about their condition. Such a patient will "contemplate his coming end with a certain degree of quiet expectation" (112), with emphasis on the "quiet." The patient's "circle of interest diminishes," and his or her desire for visitors decreases. "This is the time," Kübler-Ross says in what is for postmodernism an ironic aside, "when the television is off" (113).

Walter J. Ong responds to electronic communication technology in *Orality and Literacy* with acceptance. Certainly Ong's response expresses "quiet expectation": *quiet* because the technology of writing rather than electronic technology is its primary concern, *expectation* because Ong sees understanding of the transition from orality to literacy as a preparation for understanding of the changes being wrought by electronic communication technology.

Ong asks us first to accept "what functionally literate human beings really are: beings whose thought processes do not grow out of simply natural powers but out of these powers as structured, directly or indirectly, by the technology of writing" (78). Here are a few of the many ways in which according to Ong the technology of writing has conditioned our thought.

a. Writing gave a "crucial intellectual advantage" (91) to the Greeks, who "developed the first alphabet complete with vowels." Such an alphabet facilitated democracy because it was "easy for everyone to learn," and facilitated internationalization because it "provided a way of processing even foreign tongues." Ong even mentions Derrick de Kerckhove's theory that a "completely phonetic alphabet" leads to increasingly abstract thought because it "favors left-hemisphere activity in the brain."

b. Writing altered the way humans perceive time. "Before writing was deeply interiorized by print, people did not feel themselves situated every moment of their lives in abstract computed time of any sort" (97). Timekeeping devices like clocks and calendars were motivated at least in part by the need for written texts to be located in time as part of their validation. There was no corresponding need for oral witnesses, who, being present, could defend themselves.

c. Writing made possible charts, lists, and tables. "Primary oral cultures commonly situate their equivalent of lists in narrative, as in the catalogue of ships and captains in the *Iliad*—not an objective tally but an operational display" (99). Sequences presented in primarily oral cultures differ from sequences presented in functionally literate cultures: the items involved are perceived not as things, but as "occurrences in time, impossible to 'examine' because they are not presented visually but rather are utterances which are heard." Writing, Ong says, "reduces sound to space."

d. Print technology (an intermediate step between writing itself and contemporary electronic technology) made modern science possible. Printing made possible precision in conveying systematic information: "a sprig of white clover copied by a succession of artists unfamiliar with real white clover can end up looking like asparagus" (126). In turn, verbalization of "complex objects and processes" became more precise. This "conjuncture of exact observation and exact verbalization" is the distinctive feature, Ong says, of modern science. "The resulting hypervisualized noetic world was brand new" (127).

e. Print also helped to create "the sense of personal privacy that marks modern society" (130). As books became small and affordable, they lent themselves to "solo reading in a quiet corner" (131), unlike the social nature of oral communication and the practice of reading to a group, common in early manuscript culture. Concomitantly, print "created a new sense of the private ownership of words," setting the stage for the concept of poetry as originary or "creative" rather than redactive, and for the concept of plagiarism.

Ironically, the changes being fostered by electronic technologies are, according to Ong, in some respects a return. Although the "electronic transformation of verbal expression" only "deepened the commitment of the word to space initiated by writing and intensified by print," it also "brought consciousness to a new age of secondary orality" (135). This secondary orality resembles primary orality "in its participatory mystique, its fostering of a communal sense, its concentration on the present moment, and even its use of formulas" (136), although secondary orality is more "self-conscious" and "programmatic" in its possession of these traits.

By showing that Western noesis has altered significantly over time, and that modern noesis is conditioned in large part by the technologies of writing and print, Ong prepares us to acknowledge and accept the major noetic changes being brought on by electronic technologies. He finds four of the "objections commonly urged today against computers" (79) analogous to those urged by Plato against writing. First, computers pretend "to establish outside the mind what in reality can only be in the mind." Second, they weaken the mind by depriving it of "the work that keeps it strong." Third, computers are unresponsive, as reflected in what is by now a cliché: "garbage in, garbage out." Fourth, computers, like writing, cannot defend themselves, but are "passive, out of it, in an unreal, unnatural world."

Ong next observes that such objections cannot be communicated without contradiction. To make these objections "effective, their proponents articulate them in articles or books printed from tapes composed on computer terminals. . . . Once the word is technologized, there is no effective way to criticize what technology has done with it without the aid of the highest technology available" (80). On Ong's view, though, the situation for the critic of technology is even worse: not only the communication to others of antitechnology arguments, but the very formulation of the arguments themselves, is impossible without the aid of the technology being criticized. "The new technology is not merely used to convey the critique: in fact, it brought the critique into existence." Technology, like death, cannot even be defied: it must be accepted.

If acceptance of the "postmodern condition" justifies the label, Camille Paglia deserves the epithet *postmodern* more than most of those at whom she so frequently directs her vituperation. Like Ong, Paglia sees video culture as a return to oral tradition (Paglia and Postman 51). For her, media technologies like television are simply another occasion for "the latent paganism of western culture" to "burst forth again in all its daemonic vitality" (1991:25). Elvis is no different from Lord Byron. This particular paganism is continuous with all its previous historical manifestations. Paglia understands that the manner of our perception and activity is changing, made more intuitive and less ratiocinative by television, but on her view the transition is between states of equal value, and is therefore insignificant. Media technologies cannot alter the pervasiveness of decadence, so for her nothing impedes our acceptance of them.

Like Socratic thought, postmodern theory is, in part, grief over the losses from the technologically induced metamorphosis of a culture. But Socrates was not content with lamenting loss; through his life—and his death—he transformed the ideal of arete from Homer's *prowess* to Plato's *virtue*. It remains to be seen whether any postmodern theorist will have the force of character to forge such a powerful ideal for our new situation and our new selves.

3 Postmodern Aporesis

> *You know I say nothing to him, for he understands not
> me, nor I him.*
> —*Shakespeare*, The Merchant of Venice

In the first paragraph of his "Preface" to *The Differend*, as
terminology for addressing the dilemma of postmodernity, Jean-
François Lyotard distinguishes between "a litigation" and "a differend." In a litigation, a single rule of judgment governs the arguments
of all disputants, but a differend "cannot be equitably resolved for
lack of a rule of judgment applicable to both [or all] arguments. One
side's legitimacy does not imply the other's lack of legitimacy.
However, applying a single rule of judgment to both in order to settle their differend as though it were merely a litigation would wrong
(at least) one of them." Lyotard's distinction between two kinds of
disputes allows him to distinguish between two kinds of moral mis-
fires: *damages*, which occur within a "genre of discourse," and are
therefore "reparable according to [the] rules" of that genre, and *a
wrong*, which results from judging one genre of discourse by the
rules of another. The problem, Lyotard argues, is that differends,
and therefore wrongs, are inevitable. A litigation must ultimately
become a differend, because "a universal rule of judgment between
heterogeneous genres is lacking in general" (xi).

Lyotard correctly identifies the differend as the problem of postmodernity, but we would be wrong to treat the problem as unique to
our time. The dilemma of postmodernity has a history, and its history
is the history of philosophy. Whether as drama or as doctrine, Western
discourse has always suffered from the problem of incommensurability Lyotard finds in postmodern discourse and labels the differend.

Plato poses the problem as drama in the mythos of Socrates'
trial, where discursive incommensurability determines the course of

events. Socrates acknowledges the problem at the beginning of the *Apology*, first by stating his intention to speak the truth in a situation where he knows the jury will not heed it, and second by formulating his recognition that the jury has made up its mind already. It is the earlier accusers, "the people who took hold of so many of you when you were children and tried to fill your minds with untrue accusations against me" (18b), none of whom are present at court, against whom Socrates must defend himself. Socrates' argument is futile. In form and content alike, nothing his "genre of discourse" will allow him to say is commensurable with the jury's genre of discourse. No rule of judgment mediates between them. To juxtapose a Platonic and a Lyotardian distinction, Socrates' situation has the *appearance* of a litigation, but is in *reality* a differend. Discursive incommensurability structures the drama of the *Crito* as well. To be true to his own discursive genre, conditioned by what he considers rationality and integrity, Socrates must appeal to the law for the decision on whether or not to escape. But it is precisely the law that has condemned him. Like Job trying to take the Legislator to court, the verdict on Socrates' inquiry is fixed before the inquiry begins. Again, the appearance of a litigation (dialogue) only covers the reality of a differend (the tyranny of one discursive genre).

Shakespeare's *Merchant of Venice* also dramatically enacts discursive incommensurability. Its comic moments often result from differends, as when Bassanio and Shylock are negotiating the terms of the loan, and Bassanio misunderstands Shylock's use of the word *good*: Shylock acknowledges that "Antonio is a good man," by which he means that Antonio has sufficient money to cover the loan. Bassanio, offended at what he takes to be a questioning of Antonio's moral character, asks "Have you heard any imputation to the contrary?" Bassanio can hear only his own discursive genre, even in Shylock's words. Like its comic moments, the play's serious moments enact discursive incommensurability, as in Portia's famous courtroom speech. Attempting to persuade Shylock the Jew to be merciful, Portia the Christian insists that mercy "is an attribute to God himself." She says that "in the course of justice, none of us / Should see salvation," and assumes that "we do pray for mercy." But this is another differend masquerading as a litigation: for Shylock, mercy is at best a secondary attribute of God's, governed by God's justice. In Shylock's discourse, no ideal corresponds to Portia's Christian "salvation," and one is more likely to pray for justice than for mercy.

Of course, discursive incommensurability also enacts itself as drama in postmodern texts. In contrast to *The Merchant of Venice*, where the incommensurable discourses create the drama, in Donald Barthelme's short story "The Explanation" the drama creates the incommensurability. The audience of *The Merchant of Venice* knows prior to the play that the discourses of Judaism and Christianity are, at least on the theme of mercy and justice, incommensurable. But in "The Explanation" the audience knows nothing about the discourse of either Q or A beyond what the story leads them to posit. The differend is signalled by the discontinuity in the dialogue, in which Q asks about the machine, a black square, "Now that you've studied it for a bit, can you explain how it works?" "Of course," A replies, to which Q asks, with no apparent connection, "Is she still removing her blouse?" (37). The story contains passages like this one:

Q: She sang and we listened to her.
A: I was speaking to a tourist.
Q: Their chair is here.
A: I knocked at the door; it was shut.
Q: The soldiers marched toward the castle.
A: I had a watch (39).

By such discontinuities, Barthelme manages to create a story in which, not only are the discursive genres of the characters incommensurable with each other, but the discourse of the story is incommensurable with that of the audience.

As doctrine, Plato poses the problem of discursive incommensurability in the allegory of the cave. There the discourses of those who have seen the sun and those who have not are incommensurable. As long as all the subjects are bound in the cave, they share a discursive genre, but anyone who leaves learns an incommensurable discourse. When the enlightened person returns to the cave after sight of the sun, "would he not provoke laughter, and would it not be said of him that he had returned from his journey aloft with his eyes ruined and that it was not worth while even to attempt the ascent?" (517a). The enlightened person is wiser, but an unenlightened person, one who does not share the same discursive genre, cannot recognize the fact. Even worse, the enlightened person cannot be confident of her own enlightenment. In its temporary blindness and its proscription of what one can see, the experience of the transition from darkness to light replicates the transition from light to darkness; consequently, one cannot justify confidence in either state. One can know only that one has a *different* discursive genre, but not that one has a *better* one. Socrates narrates the story as if one could be confident in the reality of experience in light, but since he occupies the place in Plato's narrative not of a person in transition, but of a resident of light, his feeling of confidence is, like the residents of the light in the story, naivety. No rule of judgment can mediate between the discourse of those bound in the cave and those who have been outside it.

Similarly, Thomas Hobbes's *Leviathan* invokes discursive incommensurability as doctrine almost contemporaneously with its invocation as drama in *The Merchant of Venice*. As in Shakespeare's play, the differend is a religious one; in *Leviathan*, though, the issue is incommensurability, not between competing human discourses about the divine, but between divine discourse and human discourse. "When God speaketh to man, it must be either immediately; or by mediation of another man, to whom he had formerly spoken immediately." The second alternative cannot be successful, since "if a man pretend to me, that God hath spoken to him supernaturally, and immediately, and I make doubt of it, I cannot easily perceive what argument he can produce, to oblige me to believe it." That leaves only the first alternative, but no compulsion to believe attends even immediate revelation, since the methods available, "Dreams, Visions, Voice, and Inspiration," could each be misleading. There is thus for Hobbes no certainty "of knowing the will of God, by other way than that of Reason." In other words, we can hope to divine the content of God's discourse only from within our own. No rule of judgment mediates *between* divine and human discourse, since the only rule of judgment lies *within* human discourse.

Just as Lyotard's postmodern contemporaries have participated in the articulation as drama of discursive incommensurability, so his contemporaries have, like Lyotard himself, articulated the differend as doctrine. To take only the most obvious example, no philosopher has given us so manifold a vocabulary for addressing discursive incommensurability as Jacques Derrida, who uses terms like the *trace*, the *supplement*, *under erasure*, *dissemination*, the *parergon*, and *originary delay* to describe discourses not only as sometimes incommensurable with each other, but also as always incommensurable each with itself. Significantly, *différance*, the term designating his most cogent formulation of discursive incommensurability, shares its root with Lyotard's term. Instead of locating the unbridgeable gap between discourses, as does Lyotard, Derrida locates it within discourses, in two ways. First, spatially, by claiming that "the signified concept is never present in and of itself" (1982:11), but is separated from itself by différance. Second, temporally: "An interval must separate the present from what it is not in order for the present to be itself, but this interval that constitutes it as present must, by the same token, divide the present in and of itself" (13). For Derrida, no rule of judgment can make a discursive genre commensurable with itself.

So-called postmodern theorists are not the only philosophers to articulate the differend as doctrine, however. Stanley Cavell, for instance, names the differend "intellectual tragedy" as part of his commentary on Wittgenstein in *The Claim of Reason*. Cavell distinguishes between *criteria* and *standards*: "criteria, we might say, determine whether an object is (generally) of the right kind, whether it is a relevant candidate at all, whereas standards discriminate the degree to which a candidate satisfies those criteria" (11). At a contest like a dog show, the criteria are given (basset hounds must have floppy ears and thick muzzles) and the judgment consists in applying standards (this basset hound has floppier ears and a thicker muzzle than that one). Cavell claims that only on the basis of criteria can evaluations be rational, thus modifying a view he attributes to Wittgenstein: "all our knowledge, everything we assert or question (or doubt or wonder about . . .) is governed not merely by what we understand as 'evidence' or 'truth conditions', but by criteria" (14). The problem with criteria is that they must be shared in order to make reason possible, but some humans do not share criteria. In Wittgenstein's words, "One human being can be a complete enigma to another." In Cavell's words, "if the disagreement persists, there is no appeal beyond us, or if beyond us two, then not beyond some eventual us. There is such a thing as intellectual tragedy" (19).

Mysticism has long declared itself a haven safe from the differend. Introjecting the conflicting discourses into a single person transforms their incommensurability, it says, into the benign form of paradox, and results not in conflict but in edification. Takeshi in Pynchon's *Vineland* takes this approach when he wonders whether DL will "make of his life a koan, or unsolvable Zen puzzle, that would send him purring into transcendence" (180). But mysticism does not solve the problem Lyotard addresses. The differend is an interpersonal conflict in part because it is an intrapersonal conflict.

"The differend is the unstable state and instant of language wherein something which must be able to be put into phrases cannot yet be. This state includes silence," the state mysticism mistakenly believes to have escaped the perils of discourse (13). The differend is no less inevitable just because the litigation has not yet appeared in public. A differend is a conflict between discursive genres, not between people per se. *Hamlet* shows as drama what Freud shows as doctrine, that a differend within a person can kill no less than can a differend between people, and that a differend within a person cannot fail to become a differend between people.

Incommensurability takes a form conditioned by the concerns of an age: it was alethic for the ancients, preoccupied as they are with distinguishing true from false; metaphysical for the medievals, for whom the condition for valid human understanding would be coincidence with divine understanding, but who cannot communicate with God because, as Augustine puts it, "my soul's house is too narrow for you to enter" (I, 5); epistemic for the moderns, who pitch necessary postulates and pineal glands into the hungry Humean skeptical maw between noumena and phenomena, mind and body; religious for the late moderns, whose Abrahams cannot explain their Gods' murders, and whose madmen cannot explain their Gods' deaths; psychological by the fin de siècle, when the unconscious procured its own dreamy patois; lexical by the time the first world war silenced Wittgenstein; and semiotic for us postmoderns, since our signs signify only each other. Incommensurability will not go away, because, as Baudrillard puts it, "the world is not dialectical—it is sworn to extremes, not to equilibrium, sworn to radical antagonism, not to reconciliation or synthesis" (1990b:7). Like the soul Socrates imagines in the *Phaedo*, the differend's refusal to go away means, a fortiori, that it was always here. Nothing is new under the sun, or here in the cave.

4 Postmodern Freedom

Ay, marry, now my soul hath elbow-room.
—Shakespeare, King John

Human freedom cannot mean to a citizen of the late twentieth century what it meant to a citizen of the mid-nineteenth. Autonomous volitional causality makes no sense in a time when scientists have so expanded the range of possible effects from a single cause that "a butterfly stirring the air today in Peking can transform storm systems next month in New York" (Gleick 8), when psychiatrists treat emotional disturbances by chemical means, when the stock market fluctuates in response to trading performed by computers, and when by statistics advertising agencies and governments can accurately predict behavior. In an age when we can map and medically modify mental functions, an age of artificial intelligence and robotics, the old concept of freedom is anachronistic. The pony express in this age of the fax is not more obsolete. Like Newtonian mechanics, though, the old concept lingers: revolutions are effected in pursuit of the liberty to enact it, and judicial systems are predicated on humans' having it. But just as physicists since Newton have had to alter the concepts of time and space to incorporate phenomena like electromagnetism and subatomic particles, so philosophers must alter the concept of freedom. No longer can freedom be the transcendental ability of the reason that in Kant can determine a will unconditioned by the empirical, or the self-certainty of self-consciousness that in Hegel constitutes both the real and the supersensible world: belief in such freedom is the twentieth-century version of Pelagianism, the fifth-century heresy that insisted humans were free to *choose* good, in spite of God's omnipotence.

Premonitions of freedom's metamorphosis occurred long before the metamorphosis itself. Hobbes, for instance, writing more than a

century before Kant or Hegel, makes a special point of defining freedom ("absence of Opposition") in such a way that it is compatible
with necessity ("every act of mans will, and every desire, and inclination proceedeth from some cause, and that from another cause").
The transition itself, though, had to wait for the modernists. In particular, Nietzsche and Wittgenstein, by denying the existence of
freedom, caused a philosophical crisis that enforced the metamorphosis. The denial of freedom precipitated a crisis, because moral
judgments have always depended on the assumption that the agent
being judged, or the agent responsible for the action being judged, is
free. Even an apparent exception like Calvinism does not deny freedom: it only attributes responsibility for the action to a different
agent, God rather than a human.

On the infrequent occasions when they have tried to justify
the assumption that humans possess free volition, ethicists have
offered innocent-looking, pragmatically based *modus tollens* arguments like this one: (1) Without free human volition, ethical judgments are meaningless. (2) Ethical judgments are not meaningless. (3)
Therefore, there is free human volition. Nietzsche and Wittgenstein,
however, recognize that premise (2) is ungrounded. In fact we do
make ethical judgments and we do want them to be meaningful,
but our desire for meaningful ethical judgments will not make them
exist any more than my desire for the money to pay this month's
mortgage will make it appear in my bank account. Nietzsche and
Wittgenstein, then, discard both the claim that human volition is
free and the claim that ethical judgments are meaningful.

Although Nietzsche's denial of freedom appears often in his
works, a paradigmatic account occurs in *Twilight of the Idols*, as
"The Four Great Errors." Nietzsche calls the first great error "the
error of confusing cause and effect" (1968a:492). By this he means
that earlier religions and moralities held that virtue causes happiness. In fact, claims Nietzsche, virtue is not the cause but the effect
of happiness. The error itself is: "Do this and that, refrain from this
and that—then you will be happy! Otherwise . . ." (493). Nietzsche's
correction is that "a well-turned-out human being, a 'happy one,'
must perform certain actions and shrinks instinctively from other
actions; he carries the order, which he represents physiologically,
into his relations with other human beings and things."

For Nietzsche there are at least two corollaries. First, bad
actions do not damage agents, but instead damaged agents produce
bad actions. For example, instead of license and luxury destroying a

generation, Nietzsche says, "when a people approaches destruction, when it degenerates physiologically, then license and luxury follow from this." Second, what is good is "natural" rather than enforced. This directly, if tacitly, argues against Kant's view that in order for an agent to be morally praiseworthy, that agent must act solely from duty. It is not enough to do what duty commands; one must do what duty commands because duty commands it. One must act against one's inclination. In place of this, Nietzsche says, "all that is good is instinct—and hence easy, necessary, free. Laboriousness is an objection" (494). Or "in my language: light feet are the first attribute of divinity." In other words, he reverses what the moral terms "labor" and "ease" signify: labor once signified moral strength, but now signifies moral weakness; ease once signified moral weakness, but now signifies moral strength.

Nietzsche's proposed correction of this error changes human ethical agency in two ways. First, it makes morality internal instead of external. Even nominally internal moral criteria are usually ultimately external: moral intuition, for instance, does not mean that the moral law is in the individual, but that the individual does not need the mediation of any other individual or force (like the application of reason or the exposition of the law) to ascertain the moral law, which is still external to it; and Kant's "subjective necessity" is an instantiation of objective necessity. For Nietzsche, the nominally internal criteria are really internal.

Second, Nietzsche's correction places the individual under a new kind of necessity: the necessity of cause instead of the necessity of obligation. In other words, were Nietzsche's correction of the error of confusing cause and effect reformulated as the claim that, instead of its being the case that one must do what one ought to do, now one ought to do what one must, the formulation would equivocate on the word *must*. The first *must* is the necessity of obligation: although one has the power and freedom to disobey a rule, it subjects one by the sanction that disobedience will damage one. The second *must* is the necessity of cause, according to which a rule subjects one because it determines one's actions, and one has not the power or freedom to disobey. For Nietzsche, the second *must* governs morality.

The second great error, "the error of a false causality," consists in the belief that human agents are "causal in the act of willing" (494). According to this mistaken view, "all the antecedents of an act, its causes, were to be sought in consciousness and would be found there once sought—as 'motives.'" The justification for the view is that otherwise "one would not have been free and responsible" for the action. Nietzsche corrects this error by asserting that "there are no mental causes at all" (495). Consciousness, motive, will, and ego all disappear as participants in the causation of human actions. Concomitantly, freedom and responsibility disappear as characteristics of human agency.

For Nietzsche this makes the ethical agent not the locus of final causation, but at most a proximate cause. All actions occur within a causal chain, but the chain of causation does not stop at the individual's freedom. Just as *God* in Aquinas's proof merely names an arbitrary stopping point for the chain of physical causes, so *freedom* according to Nietzsche merely names an arbitrary stopping point for the chain of causes of human actions.

The third great error, "the error of imaginary causes," consists in the belief that we must have a reason for states of feeling: "we want to have a reason for feeling this way or that—for feeling bad or for feeling good. We are never satisfied merely to state the fact that we feel this way or that: we admit this fact only—become conscious of it only—when we have furnished some kind of motivation" (496). We produce imaginary causes because an explanation of a thing helps to alleviate fear of it. What earlier in *Twilight* Nietzsche calls the "principle of 'faith'" elucidates the ability of causal explanation to alleviate fear: "whoever does not know how to lay his will into things, at least lays some meaning into them: that means, he has the faith that they already obey a will" (469). Or, as the conscientious man in *Zarathustra* puts it, "fear is the original and basic feeling of man; from fear everything is explicable, original sin and original virtue" (414).

Bad feelings, attributed to "bad" causes such as hostile beings (evil spirits, devils, witches) or condemnable acts, function as punishments. Good feelings, produced by "good" causes, such as trust in God or consciousness of good deeds, function as rewards. Although Nietzsche does not explicitly propose a solution to this error, the implicit solution is clear enough: simply stop the misattribution, and begin to accept the feelings without an accompanying causal explanation.

The last of the four great errors, "the error of free will," results from "the instinct of wanting to judge and punish," and was originated by "the priests at the head of the ancient communities," who wished to reserve to themselves the right to act on this instinct.

"Men were considered 'free' so that they might be judged and pun-
ished—so that they might become guilty." According to this error,
acts "had to be considered as willed," and their origin "had to be
considered as lying within the consciousness" (499-500). This,
Nietzsche's most direct response to the assumption that normative
ethical judgments apply only to voluntary actions, comes with a
twist. Typically, the assumption of freedom *restricts* normative judgments: only if the action is voluntary is the agent responsible. On
Nietzsche's analysis it *facilitates* normative judgments: if the action
is considered voluntary, then the agent can be held responsible. As
his solution to the problem presented by the error of free will,
Nietzsche proposes to abolish the concept of guilt and the practice of
punishment. "'Enemy' you shall say, but not 'villain'; 'sick' you
shall say, but not 'scoundrel'; 'fool' you shall say, but not 'sinner'"
(150).

The four great errors share a psychological function. They allow
an individual to manipulate with no limitations the imputation of
ethical responsibility in any way convenient to that individual: to
diffuse it, to deflect it from oneself, to direct it toward another (or
others), and so on. That they accomplish this purpose explains our
interest in continuing to commit them, but does not legitimate
them. It only makes our distortion of ethical agency by means of
them a systematic rather than an accidental distortion. This systematic and uninhibited manipulation of ethical causality can be
stopped, according to Nietzsche, by considering human actions as
determined: this removes causality from humans, and so prevents its
being marshaled against some humans by others. If human actions
are determined, the grounds for judging and punishing have been
removed.

Nietzsche formulates "what alone can be *our* doctrine" in this
way: "No one *gives* man his qualities—neither God, nor society,
nor his parents and ancestors, nor he himself. . . . No one is responsible for man's being there at all, for his being such-and-such, or
for his being in these circumstances or in this environment. The
fatality of his essence is not to be disentangled from the fatality of
all that has been and will be" (500). As long as the cause of an individual's ethical qualities can be isolated from other causes either by
attributing it to a personality (God, the individual herself) or by
locating it in some entity conceived as separate from other causality
(society), as long as the ethical qualities remain separate from the
individual's essence or nature—as long, in other words, as they

retain the character of a gift—they carry with them responsibility. As long as one is separate from the whole, one's worth is questionable. So Nietzsche argues that we must say instead: "one is necessary, one is a piece of fatefulness, one belongs to the whole, one is in the whole." Then "there is nothing which could judge, measure, compare, or sentence our being, for that would mean judging, measuring, comparing, or sentencing the whole" (500-501), and as he says earlier in *Twilight*, "the value of life cannot be estimated" (474). Because ethical actions are determined, "nobody is held responsible any longer," and on Nietzsche's view "that alone is the great liberation" (501).

Since Copernicus the awareness has been forcing itself insistently on Western thinkers that, contrary to the views expressed in Psalm 8 and the creation stories in Genesis, humans do not occupy a place above the rest of the world and just below God in a hierarchy marked by qualitative distinctions. Among Nietzsche's contemporaries, this awareness found expression in the form of natural history, so that Darwin could write a book the purpose of which was to show that "man must be included with other organic beings in any general conclusion respecting his manner of appearance on this earth" (389). "The mental faculties of man and the lower animals do not differ in kind, although immensely in degree" (513). Yet until Nietzsche the taboo on applying that awareness to ethics remained. So Darwin in the same book argued that a human without social [moral] instincts "would be an unnatural monster" (483), that "moral tendencies" are transmitted genetically (492-93), and that moral qualities "tend slowly to advance and be diffused throughout the world" (498) by the principle of natural selection. Nietzsche simply took the awareness that humans are natural rather than supernatural to its logical ethical conclusion.

One might object that the changing ideas about nature suggested by twentieth-century physics render obsolete Nietzsche's claim. But to say, as I contend Nietzsche says, that human actions are subject to the laws of nature does not limit one to any particular understanding of those laws. The point is not what the laws are, but that we are subject to them, whatever they are. If a volcano erupts, to blame the volcano or describe the eruption as ethically bad would be meaningless whether one accepts Newtonian mechanics or quantum theory or relativity. Human actions, like the volcano, are according to Nietzsche subject to natural laws and therefore amoral, whatever those natural laws are. Twentieth-century physics appears to me to enforce more strictly than ever a rigid determinism. Even if principles like Heisenberg's undercut determinism, they do so by affirming the early Wittgenstein's view that actions are accidental.

Wittgenstein addresses ethics in the *Tractatus* in the propositions between 6.4 and 6.5. The thesis to be defended is 6.4: "All propositions are of equal value." This amounts to saying that propositions do not have value, since value can exist only where there is difference of value. As in Nietzsche, the change in values results from a change in causality. Wittgenstein offers this as his explanation of the meaning of 6.4:

> 6.41   The sense of the world must lie outside the world. In the world everything is as it is, and everything happens as it does happen: *in* it no value exists—and if it did exist, it would have no value.
>
> If there is any value that does have value, it must lie outside the whole sphere of what happens and is the case. For all that happens and is the case is accidental.
>
> What makes it non-accidental cannot lie *within* the world, since if it did it would itself be accidental.
>
> It must lie outside the world.

At least two comparisons can be made with Nietzsche's conclusions in "The Four Great Errors." First, Nietzsche makes the holistic claim that no part of the world has a value different from the value of the world, and the value of the world is in the world. Wittgenstein agrees that no part of the world has value in itself apart from the value of the world, but his is the atomistic claim that therefore the world as a whole has no value. Any value that exists does not exist in the world. Second, Nietzsche shares with Wittgenstein the view that "in the world everything is as it is, and everything happens as it does happen," but he draws from this the inference that what happens is necessary. Wittgenstein infers instead that what happens in the world is accidental.

There is a context for Wittgenstein's inference. The ethical question in 6.4-6.5 he formulates in causal terms, and the issue of causality has been broached already in 6.3: "The exploration of logic means the exploration of *everything that is subject to law*. And outside logic everything is accidental" [Wittgenstein's italics]. Wittgenstein in this way excludes the voluntary from the domain of possibility. Everything is either determined or accidental. "Either an event occurs or it does not: there is no middle way" (5.153). That is, if anything is subject to natural law, then according to Wittgenstein everything is. The laws of nature explain "*according to a single plan* all the *true* propositions that we need for the description of the world*" (6.343, first italics mine). One who maintains the concept of natural law cannot meaningfully maintain even the possibility of exceptions. So Wittgenstein says:

6.36   If there were a law of causality, it might be put in the following way: There are laws of nature.

But of course that cannot be said: it makes itself manifest.

6.361   One might say, using Hertz's terminology, that only connexions that are *subject to law* are *thinkable*.

The problem is (as 6.342 indicates) that the possibility of description tells nothing about the object being described (in this case the world). He has argued above that everything is either necessary or accidental; now he says that nothing in the world is necessary. Necessity is merely logical.

6.37   There is no compulsion making one thing happen because another has happened. The only necessity that exists is *logical* necessity.

6.371   The whole modern conception of the world is founded on the illusion that the so-called laws of nature are the explanations of natural phenomena.

So (1) everything is either necessary or accidental; (2) nothing except logic is necessary; therefore, (3) nothing human ethical agents do is necessary, everything they do is accidental. "The world," in other words, "is independent of my will" (6.373).

The obvious objection to this view says that human actions do not "seem" or "feel" accidental, and that our ability to offer explanations of our actions reflects the way they do seem or feel. Although Wittgenstein does not counter this objection in the *Tractatus* itself (indeed he seldom counters any objections in that gnomic work), there are ways to do so, and Wittgenstein himself suggests one in his later *Lectures and Conversations*. There he makes a distinction between cause (objective natural laws by the agency of which human choices are made and decisions are performed) and motive (the subjective experience to which we would consciously attribute our behavior). One can know the motives for one's actions, but not the causes of them. "Unless you lie you are supposed to be able to tell [in a law court] the motive of your action. You are not supposed to know the laws by which your body and mind are governed" (21). The same distinction appears elsewhere, for instance at page 15 of the *Blue Book*: "Of the cause one can say that one can't know it but can only conjecture it. On the other hand one often says: 'Surely I must know why I did it' talking of the motive." He concludes: "The double use of the word 'why', asking for the cause and asking for the motive, together with the idea that we can know, and not only conjecture, our motives, gives rise to the confusion that a motive is a cause of which we are immediately aware, a cause 'seen from the inside', or a cause experienced.—Giving a reason is like giving a calculation by which you have arrived at a certain result." The explanations we give, then, only appear to be causal, but in fact reveal motives, not causes, and therefore do not preclude the actions' being accidental. Wittgenstein's illustration is this: "'Why did you write 6249 under the line?' You give the multiplication you had done. 'I arrived at it by this multiplication.' This is comparable to giving a mechanism. One might call it giving a motive for writing down the numbers. It means, I passed through such and such a process of reasoning. Here 'Why did you do it?' means 'How did you get there?' You give a reason, the road you went" (21-22). You are unable, though, to give the cause, since (at least on the view of the *Tractatus*) the action is accidental, and there is therefore no cause to be given.

A second objection would say that if we must deny that human actions can be voluntary, it would be better to believe with Nietzsche (and science) that they are determined than with Wittgenstein that they are accidental. Again, Wittgenstein has a response, given not in the *Tractatus* but in the *Lectures and Conversations*. The justification for the view that human actions are determined is the same one given (when one *is* given) for the view that human actions are voluntary—namely, that we must suppose it to be the case: there must be laws governing human actions, although we do not know what they are. That ignores the only evidence, though—namely, that we have not discovered any laws even though we have been looking for them. So in a conversation with Rush Rhees about Freud, Wittgenstein said:

Suppose you want to speak of causality in the operation of feelings. "Determinism applies to the mind as truly as to physical things." This is obscure because when we think of causal laws in physical things we think of *experiments*. We have nothing like this in connexion with feelings and motivation. And yet psychologists want to say: "There *must* be some law"— although no law has been found. . . . Whereas to me the fact that there *aren't* actually any such laws seems important. (42)

The two premises that (1) only what is subject to law is thinkable, and (2) actions are accidental lead Wittgenstein to the conclusion that "it is impossible for there to be propositions of ethics" (6.42), which is a specific form of the more general claim that immediately follows it: "Propositions can express nothing that is higher" (6.42). Ethics, Wittgenstein believes, "cannot be put into words" (6.421). As with Nietzsche, ethics disappears because the will disappears. In Wittgenstein's words, "it is impossible to speak about the will in so far as it is the subject of ethical attributes" (6.423).

Though they disagree about the causation of human actions, Nietzsche and Wittgenstein draw similar conclusions about ethical judgments, because in terms of causation there are three possibilities for human actions, but in terms of the ethical evaluation of human actions there are effectively only two possibilities. Viewed strictly in terms of causation, human actions may be determined, voluntary, or accidental. We typically think of them as voluntary; Nietzsche argues that they are determined, Wittgenstein that they are accidental. For purposes of ethical evaluations, human actions are either voluntary or involuntary. If the actions are voluntary, ethical evaluations are meaningful; if the actions are involuntary, ethical evaluations are not meaningful. In the context of ethics, a determined action is equivalent to an accidental one: both belong to the set of involuntary actions. For this reason the critiques of volition in Nietzsche and Wittgenstein, although they suggest mutually exclusive views of the causation of human actions, have an equivalent ethical result.

Previous ethicists have disagreed about the principles according to which ethical evaluations should be made. Aristotle argued that good actions strike the mean between excess and deficiency, and that good agents acquire the habit of performing good actions and the character of desiring good things. Augustine argued that good actions are done from the motive of the love of God. Kant argued that good

actions are performed out of obedience to the categorical imperative. Bentham and Mill argued that good actions give the greatest
possible amount of pleasure to the greatest number of people. And so
on.

Nietzsche and Wittgenstein, however, make a completely different and more ambitious claim: not that there is some new ethical
principle that previous ethicists have missed, not that previous ethicists have misunderstood the basis of ethics, but that ethics has no
basis, that no meaningful ethical principle is possible. The possibility of an action or an agent having ethical value depends on the
agent's having performed the action voluntarily. Nietzsche and
Wittgenstein argue (on disparate grounds, to be sure, but with the
same effect) that humans cannot perform actions voluntarily, and
that therefore neither they nor their actions can have moral value.

Fortunately, what modernists like Nietzsche and Wittgenstein
took away with one hand, they restored with the other. They
revealed the incoherence of one idea of freedom, but in so doing
they gave us the material for another idea. If once human freedom
was like the freedom of a god, now it is like the freedom of a sign.

The philosophical roots of the semiotic concept of freedom are
most plainly visible in Marx, Nietzsche, and Freud, each of whom
began to treat human actions as signs. Treating actions as signs,
though, meant treating them as causally determined. For Marx,
human actions signify socioeconomic conditions, and are therefore
determined by the agent not as an autonomous individual but as a
functionary of history. He says, for instance, that "the functions
exercised by the capitalist are no more than the consciously and
wilfully executed functions of capital-value which valorizes itself
by absorbing living labor. The capitalist only functions as the per-
sonification of capital, capital in person, just as the worker is only
labour personified" (508). For Nietzsche, actions signify the power of
the agent, and are therefore determined by nature. In *The Will to
Power* he claims "to understand moral judgments as symptoms and
sign languages which betray the processes of physiological prosperity
or failure" (1968b:149). The strong enact their strength; the weak,
their weakness. For Freud, actions signify mental conflicts, and are
therefore determined by the unconscious processes of the agent's
mind. Because he understands psychic phenomena "as signs of an
interplay of forces in the mind, as a manifestation of purposeful
intentions working concurrently or in mutual opposition" (1977:67),
Freud considers psychical freedom an "illusion."

If the actions of a human agent are determined by forces other than the agent, then the agent does not possess freedom in the traditional sense. In fact, because the agent's activity signifies some other force, the agent is not even an agent in the traditional sense, as I and others have shown by recent studies of the "author" and "reader." My brother's advocacy of Reaganomics signifies not his having autonomously selected that point of view from a range of possibilities, but his being a white urban middle-class male; just as my dog's howling along with sirens signifies not its having deliberated before doing so, but its being a dog. Human agents, therefore, will possess freedom in whatever sense a sign possesses freedom, and signs possess freedom, as Saussure, another parent of postmodernism, tells us, in the sense that they are arbitrary. Like any other sign, then, a human agent is the locus not of volition but of arbitrariness. Because a human is part of many sign systems and simultaneously a player in many language games, what we experience as freedom and designate by the term *freedom*, I would call overdetermined arbitrariness.

By *overdetermined* I mean to express the multiplicity of signifying systems and games in which a human participates, by echoing Freud's use of the term to mean that symptoms, dream elements, or parapraxes are "determined many times over," or in other words help to express many unconscious ideas (1965:318). An action means more than one thing because I am a participant in many language games simultaneously. By *arbitrariness* I mean to follow Saussure's sense, according to which the signifier "is unmotivated, i.e. arbitrary in that it actually has no natural connection with the signified" (69). Saussure's arbitrariness has two aspects: accident and necessity. The sign is accidental in the sense that there is no reason why "sheep," instead of some other word like "ostrich," should have come to signify a woolly mammal. Yet the sign is necessary in at least the sense that it "is fixed, not free, with respect to the linguistic community that uses it. The masses have no voice in the matter," the signifier having been chosen by language itself (71). You and I cannot make "ostrich" mean "sheep," or even make "sheep" the linguistic equivalent of the French *mouton*, no matter how hard we try (115-16).

In *Elements of Semiology*, Barthes talks about freedom within language as a function of the number of combinatory possibilities. Language (*langue*) supplies constraints, and speech (*parole*) resists those constraints, with success that varies depending on the complexity of the speech. "The freedom to construct paradigms of phonemes is nil, since the code is here established by the language; the freedom to group phonemes into monemes is limited, for there are 'laws' for governing the creation of words; the freedom to combine several 'words' into a sentence is real, although circumscribed by the syntax and in some cases by submission to certain stereotypes; the freedom to combine sentences is the greatest of all" (1968a:70). Even though Barthes here slips back into the old sense of the term *freedom*, his observation that the appearance of freedom increases in proportion to the complexity of the system helps explain why the conjunction of accident and necessity peculiar to freedom feels like liberty instead of determinism. Were humans at a given time part of only one sign system, the simplicity would make determinism visible, and we would see the necessity in our behavior; the complexity brought on by being part of many sign systems submerges the necessity under the accident. Our actions feel determined when we see no alternatives or when we can isolate a single cause; where we see many alternatives or a confluence of causes, we feel control.

Viewing actions/agents as signs means replacing causality with structure as the source of their identity and meaning, or (borrowing Saussure's terms) making synchrony rather than diachrony constitutive. To the tradition, I am what I am because of my history: who my parents are, what I have done until now, and so forth. To postmodernism, I am what I am because of my context: citizen of an imperialist democracy, white male, and so forth. Tradition, in other words, views actions/agents in temporal terms; postmodernism, in spatial terms. So fundamental a revision of our self-definition calls for a new, compatible definition of freedom. Freedom in temporal terms will always be construed as in some sense a resistance to causality (whether by appropriation of causality as in Kant and Hegel, or defiance of it as in Sartre). Freedom in spatial terms must be construed instead as resistance to structure, and overdetermined arbitrariness is one way of doing so. Freedom is always freedom *for* something and freedom *from* something. The new concept of freedom I suggest does not demand a renunciation of any end for which freedom is a means (liberty, virtue, happiness, and the like). But we have learned that we are in fact not free from causality, so we must now recognize that freedom can only be freedom from structure.

On this view, freedom has the character of what Derrida calls "play." In "Structure, Sign, and Play," Derrida argues that structure has been thought of as having a center, the function of which is "to orient, balance, and organize the structure . . . but above all to make sure that the organizing principle of the structure would limit what we might call the *play* of the structure" (1978:278). There must be in every turning world a still point; there must be a fixéd foot to make the circle just. The center is called by different names, Derrida says, from *archē* to *ousia*, God to consciousness, but they have "always designated an invariable presence" (279): structure, like Donne's sublunary lovers, cannot admit absence. However, there came a moment, according to Derrida, when "language invaded the universal problematic," and when "in the absence of a center or origin, everything became discourse" (280). That "everything" includes humans. In order to establish an invariable presence, the "central signified" would have to escape the "system of differences" that is signification, and it cannot do so. In place of a center, consequently, there is play—that is, "infinite substitutions" (289). Necessity substitutes itself for accident, and accident for necessity. Neither can ground the structure of human activity, but their play is freedom. Nothing "arrests and grounds the play of substitutions." In a centered structure, there could be only accident or necessity, but not freedom. Because there is no center, we can signify; because there is no center, we are free.

Rudolf Bultmann made a living as a theologian in the 1950s by pointing out the inconsistency in a Christian's taking penicillin for strep throat while believing that Jesus healed the sick by casting out demons, and insisting on the consequent need to "demythologize" the New Testament. The analogous inconsistency between taking lithium for depression and believing that one exerts conscious, independent control over one's behavior entails a similar imperative: we citizens of postmodernity (which, like it or not, we all of us are) must demythologize the concept of freedom in order to resolve the ethical crisis posed by the modern denial of freedom.

5 Postmodern Beauty

Believe me, sir,
It carries a brave form. But 'tis a spirit.
—Shakespeare, The Tempest

In *The Inhuman*, Jean-François Lyotard denies the possibility of experiencing beauty in the computer age. In its craving to transform everything into information, he says, our age has managed to make even "so-called sensory data—colours and sounds" into digital form so that they can be "synthesized anywhere" (1991:50). From that observation he draws this conclusion: the colors and sounds

> are thereby rendered independent of the place and time of their "initial" reception, realizable at a spatial and temporal distance: let's say telegraphable. The whole idea of an "initial" reception, of what since Kant has been called an "aesthetic," an empirical or transcendental mode whereby the mind is affected by a "matter" which it does not fully control, which happens to it here and now—this whole idea seems completely out of date.

Fortunately, Lyotard, who is right his fair share of the time, is wrong about this, and he is wrong for a postmodern reason. Between the "initial reception" when Theo Van Gogh unrolled the latest painting from his brother, and my calling up the image of that painting on CD-ROM on my home computer, there is an immeasurable distance, what is variously named by postmodern theorists a gap, a difference, a remainder, a supplement, and the like. That distance is not "telegraphable," and would not be so even if the colors were.

Later in the same book, Lyotard explains why painting cannot be beautiful anymore. Photography, he says, has taken over the visible, and has therefore excluded painting from the province of the eye, leaving it "only" the province of the mind. Similarly, painting is no longer regulated by the sharable, disinterested pleasure Kant named taste, which also belongs now to photography, but by the "formless" and "negative" feeling of the sublime. Photography can now be beautiful, but painting must not be, because "when the point is to try to present that there is something that is not presentable, you have to make the presentation suffer" (125). Again, Lyotard is wrong, and again the reason can be articulated in the terminology of postmodern theory. If photography has stolen painting's potential for beauty, the theft ought to be retroactive. If new paintings cannot be beautiful for the reason that photography exists, then neither can old paintings be beautiful, since the reason (photography's existence) still holds.

The reaction to a good Van Gogh, then, must be like saying of the Katherine Hepburn of the 1980s that she is very beautiful for her age: it amounts to forgiving or overlooking a thing's anachronism. Both cases are based on mistaken assumptions: the latter, that feminine beauty is restricted to youth, and the former, that the creation of a painting is always in the past. Postmodern theory, though, besides attending to political and economic motivations that underwrite stereotypes of human beauty, has insisted with Roland Barthes that art works are eternally created here and now. There can be in beauty no anachronism to forgive. The reason can be found by reading a little farther into Kant than did Lyotard, who got through the parts on taste and the sublime, but fell asleep with the book on his lap before he got to the little section on genius.

Behind the Rijksmuseum Vincent Van Gogh in Amsterdam during the Centenary Exhibition in 1990, a temporary bank building was installed to handle tickets for the extra tourist traffic the exhibition brought. By summer, on the building's side were scrawled in black spray paint the words "This is where Van Gogh farted. f9.50 for a smell." The words were written in a hurried, unaccomplished new world hand, unlike the calligraffiti that honors the bricks of warehouses and the concrete of overpasses elsewhere in Europe, evidence that even in vandalism tradition is superiority. The building itself hardly looked like it housed a bank: a good wind or a couple of thieves with a fair-sized forklift could have taken the whole thing away. Appearances notwithstanding, it was "the bank with a red S on the window" to which one was required to go to purchase tickets to the Van Gogh Museum.

Although the museum did not open until 9:00, the queue to the bank began forming by 7:30. This branch cashed no checks and administered no loans, but was a fiduciary arm of the museum, to which it sold tickets at twenty guilders a head, about eleven dollars, or twice the price of smelling the aforementioned fart: more than other museums but still a bargain at roughly the price you would have paid that summer to eat a T-bone at Bonanza or see Bo Jackson break a baseball bat over his thigh at Royals Stadium. Each ticket specified a time before which its holder could not enter the museum. If you were not in line before 8:00, your chances of getting a ticket with a morning time were not good. And tickets could not be purchased even one day in advance: you want in tomorrow morning, you get here early. The line was seldom shorter than twenty-five people until mid-afternoon. Everyone pretended not to see the notice about the location of Van Gogh's fart, maintaining instead the embarrassed, defensive silence of the guilty, like two students catching each other cheating or teenagers both opening their eyes during a first kiss.

In front of the museum, invisible to the bank with the red S on the window, vendors sold postage stamp sets (the official Van Gogh issue, they said) and handmade greeting cards with romanticized scenes of Amsterdam on them, upscale versions of the hawkers outside Notre Dame with perforated accordions of fifty Paris postcards intended, one can only suppose, for the vacations of very popular insomniacs. During the wait between the time tourists purchased their museum tickets and the time they were permitted to enter, they took each other's picture, posing in front of the museum with one ear covered, as people pose at Pisa like they were propping up the tower.

The museum itself is a rectangular, horizontal, modern building in the middle of domino rows of seventeenth-century vertical ones. Extra parking lots have been built to accommodate the tour buses that in spite of the cost of fuel in Europe are left running no matter how long they are parked, like the Apollo rockets on millions of black and white television sets that for days before lift-off shot streams of what must have been steam. The entrance to the museum was patrolled during the centenary by a man and woman in uniform. If your ticket said 1:00 they would not let you in at 12:59. And had you asked in English for permission to shop at the bookstore while you waited until 1:00, the woman would have denied it in French, with a smile that would have made you believe you were trying to sneak into the show early even if you were not, a smile that said everybody tries that trick.

Inside, tourists could rent a Walkman with a cassette guide to the exhibition narrated in the European language of their choice or in Japanese, and into which they could even plug a second set of headphones for spouse or lover or siamese twin. A gray dais about six inches high and two feet wide kept the crowd a meter and a half from the paintings. No one stepped on it to get a closer look, although periodically a boy walked along on top of it moving his wide dust mop in continuous s-curves like the man who cleans display cases with a squeegee in the Frankfurt airport or the outline of a collar on a Rembrandt. Elderly women leaned over the dais (after butting in front of others without apologizing for, or apparently even being aware of, having been rude) to get a closer look not at the paintings but at the little placards referring to them. Art students in pairs drew hasty sketches. Parents explained "impressionism" to children in the same loud voice people use to talk to others not fluent in the language, and with the same oversimplification teachers use to describe existentialism or phenomenology or structuralism to freshmen, as if sufficient volume would ensure comprehension, and as if Van Gogh were interchangeable with Monet and Pissarro or Nietzsche with Sartre and Jaspers.

The placard below and to the left of each painting gave (in Dutch and English) the name of the painting and, in smaller letters, the current owner of the piece (many of the paintings in the exhibition being on loan from other museums and a few from private collections). Some of the paintings were mounted without extra protection from the visitors, but most were either framed under glass or mounted behind a plexiglass shield. Fortunately, the shields were not as distracting as the tinted bulletproof glass in the Louvre that hides the Mona Lisa from all but the most superficial scrutiny, ensuring that the audiences see themselves reflected in Leonardo's work more literally than he could have wished. That summer, "browsing" was discouraged: visitors were to go through the exhibition the museum's way, not try to find or make their own.

———————

The ironies in the centenary exhibition were powerful enough to justify graffiti about Van Gogh's digestive processes or to upset one's own. An internationally famous museum is devoted exclusively to the work of an artist (now by any measure the most popular painter in the world) who in his own lifetime was rejected and ignored almost completely. Behind the museum, next to the bank, a tent was set up to sell silk ties embroidered with the (now copyrighted) name of a man who never had occasion to wear a tie, and vendors got rich selling T-shirts and coffee mugs emblazoned with a self-portrait painted because the artist could not afford to hire models. Japanese businessman Ryoei Saito recently spent over eighty million dollars to purchase a painting by a man who often had to choose between buying paint and buying food. Elaborate security measures, including armed guards and electronic alarm systems, are now employed to protect paintings, many of which once were given away. Barriers now prevent viewers from touching, or even coming near, canvases that once were rolled up and sent through the public mails.

All concerned seem to be offended by one or another of these ironies, and the offense can usually be formulated in terms of desert. The offended party believes that an undeserving person or group has maltreated a deserving person. Some object that the tour group museum visitors do not deserve to identify themselves with the artist, others that the businessperson does not deserve to profit from the name of the artist, others that the artist does not deserve the attention his work now receives, and still others that the wealthy capitalist does not deserve to own the painting. Viewed from an alternative framework, however, the deserving and the undeserving need not stand in an offensive relation. The deserving and the undeserving alike can macarize rather than offend.

In his *Nicomachean Ethics*, Aristotle enumerates different kinds of friendship, distinguishing them primarily by the equality or inequality of the individuals involved. The two basic types of friendship are friendships between equals and friendships between unequals. The category of friendship between equals can be further divided. Incomplete friendships include friendship for pleasure (the kind that in high school girls with D-cups and dimples and boys with well-developed deltoids have more of than do girls with double chins and boys disfigured or dumpy) and friendship for utility (in which ambitious bank clerks become bosom buddies with bosses or nephews nurse affluent aunts). These contrast with complete friendship, the sort of friendship only an ancient Greek with a heritage of demigods and the concept of *to kalon*, indeed only a student of Plato, could consider possible. A complete friendship is the permanent mutual beneficence of two virtuous people, each unconditionally altruistic toward the other, the kind for which Elizabeth Barrett Browning later begged "If thou must love me, let it be for naught / Except for love's sake only," the kind that (without always admitting it to ourselves) we wish did exist but that we know does not.

Under the category of friendship between unequals Aristotle does not so much classify as list examples: the friendship between father and son, between an older person and a younger, between a male and a female, and between a ruler and one who is ruled. A minimum of inference, however, makes it possible to construct a classification by asking what constitutes the superiority of the one friend over the other in each of the unequal friendships Aristotle enumerates. In the case of father and son the inequality could be formulated as a difference in responsibility, in several of the senses of that term. The father shares responsibility for the son's existence, the father is responsible to care for the son until the son is an adult, the father is responsible for what the son does while under his care, and so on. In the case of older and younger, the inequality resides in experience, which Aristotle treats throughout the *Nicomachean Ethics* as not merely attended by several virtues (for example, wisdom) but as a condition for the very possibility of virtue. Males and females, on Aristotle's view, are unequal in both strength and intelligence, or to use a term general enough to cover all instances of Aristotelian ethical superiority, in capacity. Finally, the inequality between a ruler and the one ruled is power.

In a complete friendship between equals, what each friend gives to the other is of a kind with what that friend receives from the other. Aristotle identifies this shared currency as the unconditional wish for goods to the other for the other's own sake (including not only material goods, but also intangible goods like virtue and health and happiness), and active contribution toward the acquisition of those goods by the other. But friendship between unequals has no shared currency. The son cannot return to the father the same kind of friendship the father has given to the son. What the (good) ruler has done for the persons ruled cannot be repaid in kind.

Aristotle assumes without argument, because it could not have occurred to him that there would ever be any question about it, that

humans can be unequal in what I would call "magnitude of virtue."
(A slave, Aristotle would say, is capable only of "prudential virtue,"
not moral virtue, because to be moral one's actions have to make a
difference to other people. Moral actions have to matter; a slave's
actions cannot.) The American state papers embody the opposite
assumption: although persons may become rich or poor, morally
good or morally bad, they were originally, and remain in potential,
equal. Any differences in virtue between them are accidental, not
essential. In order to preserve this assumption (which is not without
benefits: by adopting it, one quickly sees through Aristotle's mistaken idea about masculine and feminine inequality) we exclude
from the realm of virtue by definition anything to which not everyone has equal access. We must not admire Herschel Walker for his
having been born a mesomorph; we must admire him for his daily
regimen of pushups and wind sprints.

This difference in assumptions makes it impossible to teach
Aristotle (or Nietzsche) to a class of nineteen-year-old Americans,
who cannot even disagree with Aristotle because they will not
understand him, but it makes possible an understanding of the relation between a great artist and that artist's audience. There are, after
all, other ways, besides responsibility, experience, capacity, and
power, that one human can be superior to another, and there are
other corresponding types of friendships between unequals. The one
the existence of which I wish here to suggest is what I would call
aesthetic friendship, in which one party is superior to the other in
vision.

———————

Van Gogh intended as pendants the pair of drawings called
"Sorrow" and "Tree Roots in Sandy Soil." In the former, a woman in
almost fetal posture sits on a low stump as though she were growing
out of it, her crossed arms resting on her knees, her forehead resting
on her forearms, her face hidden. The pencil lines that define her
contours are sharp as incisions. Her hair writhes like twisted
branches. The flowers at her feet share her sorrow the way the tro-
posphere in *Lear* contracts his neurosis. At her elbow is bramble
with blasted buds, and behind her a tiny leafless tree leans toward
her in consolation. Her breasts, the center from which the drawing
begins and to which it returns, are not the sunlit ripe pears of an
Ingres goddess, but precursors of the potatoes of the Nuenen peas-

ants: she is the Earth Mother of a barren, ruin-prone place. In the latter drawing, each branch is twisted as the joints of Yeats's "old men admiring themselves in the water." The roots of the tree in the foreground look like the arms of one skater stretching vainly toward another who has fallen through. Its multiple trunks are black, sharply outlined, imposing. The other trees in contrast are small, straight, and evanescent, so that like ghosts or human souls they might or might not be there.

Neither the consanguinity between the woman and the flora surrounding her in "Sorrow" nor the anthropomorphic animation of "Tree Roots in Sandy Soil" is the simple pathetic fallacy to which Ruskin and Eliot objected, and neither is merely an attribution of a human presence to nature, the way (as Feuerbach informs us) religious individuals, in "primitive" and monotheistic cultures alike, project their own attributes outside themselves. In each drawing, as the juxtaposition of the two underscores, the artist discovers in nature a human presence. And the discovery in these drawings is not the Sunday comics' "how many differences can you see between these two pictures" discovery, nor Freud's discovery of the shape of a vulture in the drape in da Vinci's "Madonna and Child with St. Anne." It is an eidetic presence, a synaesthetic experience for both artist and audience, the experience not of a tendentious pursuit, but of a heightened awareness. It is a human presence more vivid than the shades of a couple walking in Van Gogh's later watercolor "Town Wall," where the outlines cling to but can neither blend with nor remove themselves from the wall, like outlines of obliterated victims on the concrete of Nagasaki.

When I describe Van Gogh as superior in vision to the members of his audience, I mean it in two senses of the word vision. First, as a confluence of imagination and purpose, the sense according to which we refer to someone as a visionary. Of Van Gogh's superiority of vision in this sense, one unpersuaded by the paintings need only read the letters to Theo. One unpersuaded by the letters will not be convinced by anything I could say. In contrast, for Van Gogh's superiority in the second sense of vision, the "literal" meaning of the word, the act of seeing and what is seen, a case needs to be made.

In making that case, however, I should clarify just who I am suggesting is superior to whom. The Van Gogh of whose aesthetic friendship we are the beneficiaries and who is superior to ourselves in vision is not the historical individual who committed suicide a hundred years ago, with whom we could hardly be friends, but the "person" I called in *Morte d'Author* the "synoptic proxy": the person created as the repository of artistic intention in the interaction between a body of work by a given individual and the audience of that work. Like the god to whom I will suggest he is in some respects analogous, the Van Gogh who is superior to us never existed except discursively.

Consider, then, the "Portrait of Patience Escalier." The lines of his shoulders, the bottom edges of the brim of his hat, the top of his left forearm, and the one visible lapel of his coat (six of the eight major contour lines in the painting) all converge on the peasant's right eye, which has a solar aura exactly like that in his "Setting Sun" or like the hellish lights in "Night Café." When Vincent tells Theo that the brilliant orange background is "the full furnace of harvest" and is "like red-hot iron," he is not merely using a well-chosen figure of speech, and he is not merely engaged in symbolist gesturing. The historical Van Gogh (who, please recall, is not the person for whom I claim superior vision) saw—quite literally—the full furnace of harvest glowing like red-hot iron behind the peasant, and he saw—quite literally—in the peasant's eye the intensity of the sun.

For proof that one person *can* see in a substantially, physiologically different way than the way another sees (if simpler phenomena like colorblindness are not themselves persuasive), I appeal as an example to the experiences of the subject in A. R. Luria's *The Mind of a Mnemonist*. He, Sherashevsky, always saw and felt what he heard, and tasted and smelled what he saw, so that for him, to take one example, numbers have shapes: 6, he says, for example, is "a man with a swollen foot; 7 a man with a moustache; 8 a very stout woman—a sack within a sack" (1987:31). That Van Gogh himself experienced a similarly distinctive mode of perception is in principle impossible to prove (as it is in principle impossible to prove the existence of God, no phenomenon being sufficient), but that the proxy Van Gogh, the Van Gogh of the paintings and letters, did is, I think, difficult to deny.

Even if the paintings are insufficient evidence to tell us how the historical Van Gogh saw, they do tell us the more important fact of what the proxy Van Gogh saw, and that *his* vision possesses to a rare degree the aesthetic equivalent of Aristotle's "magnitude of virtue."

Toward the end of the *Critique of Pure Reason*, when his every available mental digit is damming a defect in that rapidly decaying dike, Kant argues that God and a future life are two postulates that, though insusceptible to proof, are made necessary by reason itself. Reason tells us we should do "that through which thou becomest worthy to be happy." God is necessary to ensure that those who deserve to be happy will be so, and a future life is necessary to ensure that, since He so seldom gets around to it in this life, God has time to make the deserving happy.

Again the issue is the deserving and the undeserving, but Kant helps to reveal the problem that, applied to aesthetic concerns, Aristotle's notion of friendship between unequals helps to solve. Note that Kant assumes in the very formulation of the issue that desert and happiness are separate, and that the deserving are therefore by definition incomplete, needing to be given happiness by some outside source. On this count, Aristotle's view is more satisfying: the deserving person is by definition whole, already by definition possesses happiness (not the mere feeling of pleasure as in Mill nor the mere ability to satisfy the insatiable desires as in Hobbes, but the state of *eudaimonia*, which even the Van Gogh who shot himself might have had), and is by definition a giver, not a receiver. In other words, Kant's concept of the deserving person *needs*, as he himself makes explicit, a higher being, while Aristotle's deserving person *is* a higher being. On Kant's view the deserving person needs to be repaid for being deserving; on Aristotle's view, the deserving person could not be repaid precisely because he is deserving. On Kant's view desert is an empty state that must be filled by happiness; on Aristotle's view desert is a full state that cannot but overflow. Kant's is a capitalist view in which goods are distributed according to desert; Aristotle's is a communist view in which goods are distributed by the deserving according to need. Kant's view accords well with the modern American love of fame, in which wealth, privilege, and the like, are concentrated by the many in the hands of the few; Aristotle's view supports his notion of magnanimity, in which, by contrast, the few disperse what is naturally concentrated in their hands.

The magnanimity in the friendship from an aesthetic superior need not be self-conscious to be magnanimity. The intention to give is not a necessary condition of giving. Public service is not restricted to public acts. There live individuals whose every act is a gift. There live individuals the mere existence of whom is a public service.

Van Gogh's parents did not assign the name Vincent first to him, but to a brother stillborn a year before Van Gogh's birth. In his early childhood, then, Vincent walked past his own grave in the churchyard every Sunday, so we should not be surprised that later when he saw his own birth (Theo and Jo having named their boy Vincent), he painted his most beautiful canvas and then fell ill. Although the presentation to the new parents of "Almond Branches in Blossom," painted in honor of their child's birth, looks altruistic, it is hardly an instance of selflessness. The usual analysis in terms of the influence on its composition of Japanese prints, and the symbolic association of blossoms with birth, although it draws attention to the sense in which the canvas *was* a gift, prevents our recognizing the more important sense in which it *is* one. So long as we think of it as an occasional piece given as one aesthetic equal might give to another, its beauty and its importance will be veiled.

Almond blossoms are not only symbolic but also allusive. Vincent, the former evangelist to the miners of the Borinage, could not have made this choice without thinking of the first vision of the prophet Jeremiah: "The word of the Lord came to me: 'What is that you see, Jeremiah?' 'An almond in early bloom,' I answered. 'You are right,' said the Lord to me, 'for I am early on the watch to carry out my purpose.'" Not, as would be the case with simple symbolism, birth in general nor even the birth of Theo's child *simpliciter* preoccupies Vincent, but the complex relationship that tranforms Theo's child's birth into Vincent's own birth: only a few verses before Jeremiah's vision is the famous passage in which God says to him, "Before I formed you in the womb I knew you for my own."

This painting is not, as catalogs describe it, unsigned: the name "Vincent" is spelled out quite clearly in the shape of the branches. If Keats wrote his name on water, Van Gogh spelled his on blue sky. This painting, with its aetherial brush strokes and infinitely rich color, is a gift from an aesthetic superior. But no imagined selflessness grounds the real magnanimity, nor does the public act of sending the canvas to his brother make it a gift; instead, the self-centered, private intensity of a great person overflows to our benefit.

To be the only audience for one's own work is easy. The difficulty is to be so because one is oneself the only individual worthy of it. The difficulty is to create work the fame of which is a diminution.

The artist aims not to delight or to teach, but to perfect and embody his isolation. The artist aims to become divine. The great artist—Van Gogh, Shakespeare, Michelangelo, Beethoven, Nietzsche—achieves this aim. Like the medieval God, the great artist is impassible, and cannot be made to suffer or to be happy by others. Like the good person of Plato's *Republic*, the great artist cannot be harmed.

The artist is solitary not because she is rejecting friendship but because she is seeking a different kind of friendship, the aim of which is not companionship but blessing. It need not occasion anger, then, that people have made of Van Gogh's work what they have. One takes from a superior what one can. One gives back to a superior what one can. Sometimes that is little. Sometimes it is nothing.

Nietzsche says in *The Will to Power*: "The sober, the weary, the exhausted, the dried-up (e.g., scholars) can receive absolutely nothing from art, because they do not possess the primary artistic force, the pressure of abundance: whoever cannot give, also receives nothing" (1968b:422). He is wrong. Because abundance *is* a pressure, whoever can give must give. But receiving is not limited to the abundant. They most need to receive, who cannot give. Indeed they have nothing to give in part because those who can give need nothing.

Each of the thousands of individuals who pass through the Van Gogh Museum in a given year receives an aesthetic friendship from a superior. None can return the friendship in equal measure, but each can experience the gratitude Christopher Smart says is grace, and can say with the speaker in W. S. Merwin's "Man With One Leaf in October Night" that "I have not deserved you."

6   Postmodern Obscenity

No, no, they would not do so foul a deed.
—*Shakespeare*, Titus Andronicus

Obscenity is vicious and pervasive, a threat to our culture significant enough to qualify as our paradigmatic vice. On that no less unlikely a pair than Jesse Helms and Jean Baudrillard agree. Over what constitutes obscenity they part company, of course, republicans (unwittingly) objecting to obscenity on grounds similar to those formulated by ancient and modern Western philosophers, with postmoderns (self-consciously) objecting to obscenity *and* the philosophical tradition. Helms is a caricature of the philosophers who could have saved him from becoming what he is; Baudrillard caricatures the philosophers whose ideas are not what they seem.

Socrates' expulsion of the poets from his imaginary republic is one of the first arguments against obscenity. Socrates spends so much of his argument establishing that mimesis can produce only appearance but never reality, and that the mimetic arts of painting and poetry are "far removed from truth," that many commentators have read the argument as if in it the crucial conflict were between appearance and reality. However, Socrates goes on to establish that the problem is not deception but corruption; not that the artist "would deceive children and foolish men" (Plato 598b), but that mimetic art "is an inferior thing cohabiting with an inferior and engendering inferior offspring" (603b).

Socrates argues in Book IV that the soul is tripartite, composed of a rational, an appetitive, and a "high-spirited" part; the rational, he says, is the superior part, and the appetitive and high-spirited the inferior parts. The problem is not just that mimetic art produces appearance instead of reality, but that in doing so it appeals "to the inferior elements of the soul." He argues in Book IX that when the inferior parts of the soul are stimulated (as by wine) and the rational part subdued, the human becomes beastly (since the only part of the soul unique to humans is the rational part), and will not refrain from "any foul deed" (571d). By an analogous argument, he says that the mimetic artist "stimulates and fosters" desire, rather than reason (605b), and thus "sets up in each individual soul a vicious constitution." Socrates considers all mimetic art obscene because "in regard to the emotions of sex and anger, and all the appetites and pains and pleasures of the soul which we say accompany all our actions, the effect of poetic imitation is the same. For it waters and fosters these feelings when what we ought to do is dry them up, and it establishes them as our rulers when they ought to be ruled" (606d).

Although Socrates is unusual for the scope of his category of the obscene, including in it all mimetic art, he sets out what will become the standard criterion for obscenity—namely, its appeal to or fostering of desire instead of reason. Obscenity is guilt by association: the association of art with the irrational. Obscenity is one way in which art can fail to meet the standard Nietzsche called (with ironic intent) "aesthetic Socratism": "to be beautiful, everything must be intelligible" (1968c:83-84).

Describing *his* republic in the *City of God*, Augustine follows Socrates in impugning desire. Agreeing in advance with Shakespeare's Edgar that "the gods are just, and of our pleasant vices / Make instruments to plague us," Augustine argues that the punishment God inflicts on humans reflects the act of disobedience that originally prompted the punishment. An eye for an eye and a penis for a penis. The soul "rejoiced in its own freedom to act perversely and disdained to be God's servant." Consequently, "it was deprived of the obedient service which its body had at first rendered" (1984:XIII, 13). In other words, as Augustine goes on to explain, God cursed humanity with desire. Before the Fall, the body was subject to the soul "in all respects"; after the Fall, the division between soul and body caused by desire so "vitiates our nature" that death is able to defeat us.

Anticipating Descartes' desperate conclusion that the jointure between soul and body must have a specific locus, the pineal gland, Augustine concentrates the division between soul and body in a specific locus, the genitals. Before the Fall, "the one part of the body" (XIV, 23) was not "activated by the turbulent heat of passion" (XIV, 26), but instead was "brought into service by deliberate use of power when the need [so to speak] arose." Adam, in other words, got a boner not because he happened to see Eve naked but because he *chose* to have one. After the Fall, erections became as involuntary, and as debasing, as a dog's wagging its tail. Sex changed as a result of the Fall; we gained the desire now associated with it and we lost the happiness in which it once participated. As a result of the Fall, lust supplanted love. Even sex within marriage has been corrupted: permission to satisfy desire does not make desire satiable; just because we *may* satisfy our desire does not mean we *can*. Sex per se is no more obscene than breathing; but just as breathing when it serves desire (as in certain telephone calls) becomes obscene, so sex's subjection to desire, by excluding the soul, renders it obscene.

Because he shares Augustine's belief that desire is body without soul, Kant (transcribing his barely sublimated Pietism) creates an entire philosophical system premised on the deracination of desire. Nowhere is this more obvious than in the Kantian opus most directly relevant to the idea of obscenity, the *Critique of Judgment.* A judgment of beauty "in which the least interest mingles," says Kant, "is very partial and not a pure judgment of taste" (1951:39). As it was for Plato and Augustine, as it will be for Jesse Helms, so is it for Kant: desire renders obscene. Aesthetic judgment must be disinterested in order to preserve its purity. Desire corrupts aesthetic judgment for Kant, just as it does for Augustine. In his aesthetics, Kant sets himself the desert island test: my judgment is pure only if, were I on a desert island "without the hope," Kant says in a felicitous translation, "of ever again coming among men" (39), and were I able to "conjure up" the item I am judging, I would not trouble myself to do so.

Kant appeals to disinterest in order to ensure that the pleasure beauty gives is uncorrupted by desire, as he appeals to the a priori in order to ensure that human knowledge is uncorrupted by perception. Disinterest is part of Kant's systematic critique of egoism: the *Critique of Pure Reason*, like the Copernican scientific theory it wishes to replicate epistemologically, argues against privileging my individual perspective in the pursuit of knowledge; the *Critique of Practical Reason*, like Kant's other moral works, argues against privileging my individual aims over those of others; and the *Critique of Judgment* argues against privileging my private longings. Kant argues against idiom: I can know only what you can also know; what is good for me must also be good for you; and what I like you must like. Kant excommunicates desire because it refuses to play by his rules, because it *is* the refusal to play by any rules except its own.

Plato, Augustine, and Kant are cornerstones of a tradition bent on extirpating desire, a tradition in which as Democritus puts it, "virtue consists not in avoiding wrong-doing, but in being without any wish for it" (Wheelwright 185). In contrast, postmodern theorists like Baudrillard and Derrida derive their views on obscenity from a tradition in which virtue consists not in being without wrong wishes, but in not wronging wishes. Thus Blake writes that "He who desires but acts not, breeds pestilence" (151), and Nietzsche that "all that is good is instinct."

If traditional views of obscenity originate in the Platonic and Judeo-Christian taboos against sexuality, the postmodern reversal of the concept of obscenity begins in the Freudian alteration of ideas about sexuality. In contrast to Kant, who rejects desire because it is idiomatic, Freud accepts the privacy and irrationality of desire. He takes as a given the "overvaluation of the sexual object," an "appreciation" that "extends to the whole body of the sexual object and tends to involve every sensation derived from it" (16). No lover will agree to Kant's demand for subjective universality in the judgment of beauty. Why should I care whether or not you consider my wife beautiful? She is beautiful to me. Nor is the lover's appreciation strictly aesthetic. "The same overvaluation spreads over into the psychological sphere: the subject becomes, as it were, intellectually infatuated . . . and he submits to the latter's judgments with credulity" (16). In the *Phaedrus*, the loss of judgment that attends desire impedes love's attainment of its ultimate goal of transcending sexuality, which is equivalent to its becoming rational. In the *Three Essays*, the loss of judgment that attends desire, by conditioning "normal" sexuality and ultimately mental health, makes love possible. "Love," as Nietzsche puts it, "is the state in which man sees things most decidedly as they are not" (1968a:591).

Consequently, in contrast to his predecessors, for whom desire's victory is our defeat, for Freud desire's defeat is also our own. Freud defines perversions as "sexual activites which either (a) extend, in an anatomical sense, beyond the regions of the body that are designed for sexual union, or (b) linger over the intermediate relations to the sexual object which should normally be traversed rapidly on the path towards the final sexual aim" (16). In other words, perversion (which for Freud is not immoral sex but unhealthy sex) is characterized by failure of penetration. For Plato, Augustine, and Kant, we are engaged in a *contest* with sexuality such that when sexuality wins, we lose. For Freud, we are engaged in a *struggle* with sexuality such that when sexuality loses, we lose.

Thanks to its origin in Freud, postmodern obscenity reverses traditional views. For Plato, obscenity begins when we foster sexuality; for Augustine, obscenity begins when we acquire sexuality; for Kant, obscenity begins when we accede to sexuality. For Baudrillard, obscenity begins when we *lose* sexuality. Like perversion for Freud, obscenity for Baudrillard results from a failure of penetration. Because "there is no longer a system of objects," nothing "existing beyond and above exchange and use" (1988:11), there is "no longer any transcendence or depth," only "a screen and a network" (12). There is, for Baudrillard, only surface. "We no longer exist as playwrights or actors but as terminals of multiple networks" (16). With the resolution into surface and circulation, "the distinction between an interior and an exterior" disappears, "blurred in a *double obscenity*" (20). The same transition that exposes "the most intimate operation of your life" also "unfolds" the "entire universe . . . unnecessarily on your home screen" (20-21).

We live in what Baudrillard calls "the ecstasy of communication," by which he means the transformation of the seen from depth to surface, substance to screen. "It is no longer the obscenity of the hidden, the repressed, the obscure, but that of the visible, the all-too-visible, the more-visible-than-visible; it is the obscenity of that which no longer contains a secret and is entirely soluble in information and communication" (22). The seen / scene changes from an object into a commodity: "the market is an ecstatic form of the circulation of goods, as prostitution and pornography are ecstatic forms of the circulation of sex" (23). The obscene does not result from desire; rather, it eliminates the possibility of desire. Obscenity harms not because it arouses us, but because it neuters us, because it renders us capable only of fascination but not of passion (26).

For Derrida, as for Baudrillard, the distinction between inside and outside has disappeared. For Derrida, as for Baudrillard, the result is obscenity. Where there is neither inside nor outside, there can be perversion, but there can be no penetration. Derrida's preference for the term *parergon*, though, signals that his preoccupation is slightly different. *Obscene* and *parergon* are (etymologically) synonymous terms, the former from a Latin root, the latter from a Greek root. Both prefixes connote ambiguity of spatial relation. Ob-, in addition to the polyvalence lent by its various nonspatial senses such as "because of," "instead of," and "in proportion to," means "before" or "in [the] front of," either of which can imply both inside-ness and outside-ness. I can stand before the crowd I am a part of, or before the pope's quarters in the snow; I can stand in the front of an auditorium or in front of a car. Similarly, para-, in addition to other meanings like "in comparison with" or "during," means "beside" or "alongside of," again with the ability to imply both inside-ness and outside-ness. I can stand beside my wife in hard times, or beside someone at the bus stop. In both words, *obscene* and *parergon*, the root denotes a locus of activity. Only the temporality has changed: the scene is where action is occurring, and the ergon is where action has occurred. Thus Baudrillard's use of *obscene* reflects his emphasis on how obscenity affects us, and Derrida's choice of *parergon* reflects his emphasis on how obscenity affects the work. In both cases, though, obscenity itself assumes the flaw that once belonged to desire: obscenity is in the work but not in it, as desire was what invaded the person, but invaded precisely as an absence, a lack.

Derrida's examination of the parergon occurs, not surprisingly, in a discussion of Kant's third critique. Derrida defines the parergon in this way: "A parergon comes against, beside, and in addition to the *ergon*, the work done, the fact, the work, but it does not fall to one side, it touches and cooperates within the operation, from a certain outside. Neither simply outside nor simply inside. Like an accessory that one is obliged to welcome on the border, on board. It is first of all the on (the) bo(a)rd(er)" (54). Following Kant, Derrida's primary examples of parerga are the frame on a painting, the clothes on a statue, and the columns on a building.

Derrida recognizes, as Kant could not, that the parergon is inevitable, but Derrida also recognizes that the parergon is a corruption, and that the malignity of the corruption varies. For Derrida, as for Plato, Augustine, and Kant, the obscene / parergon occurs at the site (sight) of a lack, but in contrast to the others, for whom the lack is a moral one and the site is ourselves, for Derrida the lack is an ontological one, "which cannot be determined, localized, situated, arrested inside or outside" (71), and the site is the work. The parergon is the limen that cannot be eliminated.

A simple comparison between Robert Mapplethorpe's 1982 "Marty and Veronica" and pages 20-21 of the Winter Sale '91 *Victoria's Secret* catalog will demonstrate the practical difference brought about by the theoretical change from a traditional conception of the obscene to what I am calling "postmodern obscenity."

The Mapplethorpe photo portrays the models as individuals, while the catalog treats models interchangeably. Such interchangeability reflects the loss of sexuality that for Baudrillard characterizes obscenity, because it replaces the Freudian overvaluation of the sexual object, in which the object is viewed (in spite of all the evidence) as incomparable. In the Mapplethorpe photo, the pose and the framing are singular. A man and woman are stylistically depicted as engaged in cunnilingus. The woman lies on her back, dressed in a black merrywidow with hose and high heels. We watch from just above and beyond her head. We see her from her breasts down, but her arms, shoulders, and head are cropped from the bottom of the photo. We see the man's arms, shoulders, and head: exactly what we do not see of the woman, no more, no less, as if the two halves of *Homo Symposium* have only now found each other after twenty-five hundred years apart. His hands hold her bent knees, her heels rest on his shoulders, and his face covers her genitals so that only the hair on the top of his head and between her legs is visible. The act depicted might be iterable, but the photo emphasizes the uniqueness of this one instance of the act. The contrast in skin color isolates each model. The ambiguity of the man's posture, neither clearly over her in an attitude of dominance nor clearly prostrate before her in an attitude of submission, is arresting. The models are even assigned proper names (ambiguous though they may be: Marty might be hypocoristic for Martha or Martin, and Veronica also names the sudarium, the handkerchief with which in Christian lore Saint Veronica is said to have wiped the bleeding face of Jesus on the road to Calvary).

In contrast, the catalog models simply give shape to the clothing they inhabit. One leans against the wall in the entrance to an elegant parlor, looking with expectation into the distance, dressed in a "full-length rayon paisley robe in jewelled blues and greens, with a touch of fuchsia," opened enough at the top to see a fair portion of one breast, and holding the bottom open to reveal one thigh all the way to the (barely) hidden genitals. Another reclines, propped on her elbows in the half-light of a window in an otherwise dark room, dressed in a purple satin and black lace bodysuit (created to defy *Tractatus* 4.002 and fitted, the accompanying text informs us, with bottom snaps), her gaze directed at the viewer. One strap has fallen off its shoulder, and a purple satin robe has fallen to her elbows. The effect of each picture would be the same were the models interchanged. We might just as well be seeing the thigh of the woman in the body suit and the shoulder of the woman in the robe. Indeed, only a few models are used repeatedly throughout the catalog, and no discernible pattern dictates who wears what or poses how.

The catalog photos are means, the Mapplethorpe photos ends. The photos in the catalog have been transformed from object into commodity, acquiescing in "ecstatic forms of circulation," not only in the obvious sense that the catalog photos exist in order to procure your money, but also in a more subtle way. The catalog pictures, because they are infinitely repeatable, lead the viewer past or through the work. They are calculated to make the viewer want to repeat them, in two ways: seeing more of them, and re-creating them (either by making oneself like the photograph, which can be done, the catalog implies, simply by ordering the apparel depicted, since the women are after all interchangeable; or by making a proximate woman approximate the women in the pictures, which can be done in the same way for the same reason). The Mapplethorpe photo-graph, instead of leading the viewer past the work, insists that the viewer stop at the work. There are no more photos like it to be seen, and because the models are singular the photo cannot be re-created. The catalog photo of the model in the body suit would be the same if the "paisley robe model" had posed in it, but the Mapplethorpe photo would be different if, for instance, "Veronica's" face were to "Marty's" genitals, or if the male model were white and the female model black.

In the catalog photos no sexual partner is present, though one is obviously needed; the photos constitute a request that the viewer provide the sexual partner (either by becoming the woman or by becoming the sexual partner). They invite fantasy. In the Mapplethorpe photo, all the requisite sexual partners are already present, already performing the act without the viewer, who is there-fore unnecessary. This photo does not invite fantasy but confronts one with reality. The catalog photos are calculated to entice the viewer to want to "do it"; the Mapplethorpe photo is calculated to force the viewer to think about it. "Everything beautiful," as Vilhelm Ekelund says, "wants to tell you something. Everything beautiful wants to become thought" (40).

Finally, the catalog photos are dominated by parerga, especially the nighties it advertises, which, like the clothing on a statue, are "not internal or intrinsic . . . to the total representation of the object," but are instead "a surplus, an addition, an adjunct, a sup-plement" (57). If the purpose of the catalog photos is sexuality, the clothing is a parergon; if the purpose of the photos is a business transaction, the models are parerga.

The elements of the settings in which the models appear are in the catalog parerga as well. On page 5 of the same (Winter Sale '91) catalog, for example, texts appear in two of the three photographs on the page, and in both cases the photos have been inverted so that the words read backward. In one, a woman gazes longingly at the viewer, wearing a pale pink cotton knit oversized "sleeptee you'll adore," its bosom "decorated with a bouquet of floral embroidery," one part of its neck (as always) drooping languidly so as to show a smoldering shoulder, fingering her hair in anticipation of whatever act the viewer is supposed to be imagining, while beside her hip is a book entitled *The Hour of the Angel*, spelled backward, perhaps (as Cincinnatians or Southern Baptists might suppose) by the same agency responsible for the subliminal Satanic messages on records by Judas Priest or Motley Crüe. In the other, a woman wears "ecru rose print" pyjamas and, presumably because the pyjamas are "too pretty to wear for just sleeping," puzzles over a newspaper. The top two buttons are undone, exposing the slope of one breast; her forehead rests on one hand, whose fingers sybaritically explore her hair; she wears glasses, but they do not help, because the headline, "ARE YOU A POOR TALKER?," is backward. In the first photo, the book is supposed to suggest, one assumes, that the woman has finished her slightly racy book but is not yet tired, and on this Eve of St. Agnes hopes the viewer will, like some Al S. in Wonderland, contrive to visit her (the mirror for his speculation is offered in the adjacent picture). In the second, the newspaper is supposed to suggest that the woman has just enjoyed an April morning in bed with the windows open (sleeping, like Descartes, until noon), and now reads the paper her lover has been through already and left rather sternly creased. What the backwardness of the texts actually suggests (like the tradition of stereotyping and repression in which the catalog participates) is that women need not read to perform their function.

In contrast, the Mapplethorpe photos contain no such parerga to disrupt or diffuse or dissemble their purpose. If Marty and Veronica needed a book, they are through with it, so it does not appear in the photograph. And even when Mapplethorpe uses props, like the frequently appearing bondage apparatus and the whip he has inserted in his anus in the 1978 "Self Portrait," they are essential to the aims of the photos, rather than inessential supplements.

In the discursive realm of Plato, Augustine, and Kant, Jesse Helms's description of Mr. Mapplethorpe as a pervert is justifiable. Yet a simple shift to the postmodern discursive realm reveals Plato and company as themselves perverts, guilty of what (by perverting one of Freud's terms) we might call "artistic scopophilia": a mutual failure of penetration in which they neither penetrate the work nor are penetrated by it. "Mere" looking has become the final aim. When one is unable to enter a work, when one is in Freud's terms a voyeur, in Baudrillard's terms ecstatic, or in Derrida's terms a parergon, one applies external standards to the work. The standard might be Arthur Danto's opinion, the amount of money paid for the work at Sotheby's, or its ubiquity in college art history texts; in the case of Plato et al., the standard is their purported morality.

Obscenity threatens art no less for postmodern theorists than for earlier philosophers and for contemporary conservatives; only obscenity for the postmoderns is characterized not by the success but by the failure of sexuality. For Plato, Augustine, Kant, and Helms, the obscene by stimulating desire invites it to devour us from without like a wild beast. For Baudrillard and Derrida, the obscene by immobilizing desire invites it to consume us from within like a cancer.

7 Postmodern Censorship

O, like a book of sport thou 'lt read me o'er;
But there's more in me than thou understand'st.
Why dost thou so oppress me with thine eye?
—Shakespeare, Troilus and Cressida

Postmodern theory stands on the recognition of a particular kind of complexity: that meanings and values always carry their opposites within themselves. To recognize that complexity, though, one must surrender a naive belief in the possibility of achieving Kierkegaard's ideal of purity of heart. One cannot will one thing without also willing its opposite, or do one thing without also opposing it, or be one thing without also being its opposite.

Traditional arguments against censorship have tacitly assumed an equation between aesthetic liberty and moral good, and therefore a purity of heart on the part of both the censoring agency and the censored party: the censoring agency by willing to restrict aesthetic liberty also wills to diminish moral good, and the censored party by willing to enact aesthetic liberty also wills to increase moral good. Thus in *Areopagitica*, the most famous argument against the regulation of publishing, John Milton treats books as pure entities able to "preserve as in a vial the purest efficacy and extraction of that living intellect that bred them." He describes them as "reason itself," the "image of God, as it were, in the eye" (720). Where books are angels, censors are demons who commit "a kind of massacre, whereof the execution ends not in the slaying of an elemental life, but strikes at that ethereal and fifth essence, the breath of reason itself."

Postmoderns have not relinquished arguments against censorship, but after the admission that (borrowing Camille Paglia's formulation) "beauty has its own laws, independent of Christian morality" (1991:116), no argument that assumes purity of intention will retain its force. Were beauty pure gain, censorship would be a simple issue. As it is, beauty is an exchange, and the price is sometimes the good. Postmoderns have had to realize that to will an increase in aesthetic liberty is sometimes also to will a diminution of moral good. Censoring agency and censored party may feel disgust for each other, but disgust is "incipient vomiting," and "what you vomit must in some way have been inside you" (Sartre 502).

That recognition may end traditional arguments against censorship, but it can be a beginning for other arguments, as Schlegel realized long before the term *postmodern* was coined. "A philosophy of poetry as such would begin with the independence of beauty, with the proposition that beauty is and should be distinct from truth and morality, and that it has the same rights as these" (53). If arguments against censorship can count as a philosophy of poetry, J. M. Coetzee begins where Schlegel recommends. The essays on censorship in Coetzee's collection, *Doubling the Point*, argue against political regulation of literary publishing, one by looking at the pornography trial of *Lady Chatterley's Lover*, and the other by evaluating arguments used to justify censorship in South Africa.

Coetzee, like Milton, argues for traditional ideals like "truth" and "freedom." Those two words so pervade contemporary political and cultural rhetoric that, having been appropriated by myriad voices in support of myriad aims, they have been emptied. Like MBAs and algebraic variables, they stand for nothing. We live in the age, after all, when tabloids proclaim "the *truth* about Elvis" and presidents advocate aid to "*freedom* fighters." What Elias Canetti says of the word "God" also holds for "truth" and "freedom": all our powerful words having been exhausted, people now say "truth" and "freedom" simply to speak words that used to be powerful. In *Doubling the Point*, though, Coetzee restores to those two words some of their lost power, and in doing so achieves the ideal Canetti describes in this way: "one comes closer to truth only in the words one no longer fully believes. Truth is a reanimation of dying words" (157).

Coetzee's reanimation of "truth" and "freedom" begins by reversing one of the processes that helped to empty them: oversimplification. He acknowledges, as Milton does not, their complexity and impurity. We love to treat truth and freedom as if we could have them in a pure state, as if they did not carry their opposites inside themselves, but as a fiction writer, Coetzee's pursuit of truth takes the form of protracted lies, and as a white South African, his freedom comes at the obvious expense of others' lack of freedom. He occupies, then, a vantage from which he could either confront with unusual intensity the impurity of the concepts of truth and freedom, or repress that impurity to an unusual extent. *Doubling the Point* grows from his having chosen the former alternative. The price of truth is a lie, and the price of freedom, oppression: Coetzee does not steer the easy course around that dilemma, but confronts it in all its complexity.

Milton makes four points in his argument: 1. Catholicism is responsible for the idea of censoring books. 2. Reading is good, regardless of the content of the books read. 3. Censorship is inevitably unsuccessful: it will not prevent the publication of the bad books it is intended to suppress, though it will frequently prevent the publication of good books. 4. Censorship inhibits learning and stanches the flow of truth. Without ever mentioning Milton or arguing directly against these four points, Coetzee shows the naivety of each, in the process of producing an even more compelling rejection of censorship.

The first of Milton's arguments is, to a twentieth-century American, a transparent appeal to the prejudice of his stated audience, members of Parliament in an England still in the springtime of its break from Catholicism. Coetzee reveals that this strategy of Milton's is infected by the frame of mind of those against whom he is arguing: censorship itself results from paranoia, and Milton's argument against censorship reflects that paranoia. "The further we explore the phenomenon of censorship," Coetzee says, "the more pivotal we find *attribution* to be, specifically the attribution of blame, and the dynamic that blaming initiates, a dynamic of blaming and counterblaming" (1992:328). The easy part, on Coetzee's view, is recognizing the paranoia in proponents of censorship (in his case, J. C. W. van Rooyen, the chair of the Publications Appeal Board in South Africa and author of two books defending South African censorship policies). The hard part is not becoming paranoid oneself. "The admit-or-condemn judgment we call censorship continues to bear, as its first and instinctive moment, a primitive incorporative-or-expulsive character" that, once present, demands a similar response from its opponents (331). It must itself be either incorporated or expelled. Sartre says that "Poetry cannot be circumscribed: if you introduce it somewhere into speech, all speech becomes poetic" (293); Coetzee says the same of censorship. Neither he nor Milton can escape the paranoia of censorship: "I place censorship under suspicion. As I place it under suspicion of hiding its true nature, of being a paranoid act, my criticism itself cannot escape from the paranoid dynamic of judging, blaming, expulsion" (1992:332).

Milton's second point usually takes the form today of the claim Coetzee watches D. H. Lawrence make: that impure minds will corrupt whatever they read, and pure minds cannot be corrupted. Coetzee's formulation of Lawrence's thesis is that "only a mind already tainted can be touched by taint" (310). If that thesis were true, though, no mind could ever *become* impure. Literature could never have a moral effect. Coetzee shows that even the "untainted" Lawrence has "a sharp nose for taint," and asks rhetorically, "Is any reading at all possible to a man without a nose? Where would such a man begin reading?" Even an argument against censorship cannot premise itself on the view that all mental corruption is already complete, and no more is possible.

Coetzee's implicit assessment of Milton's third claim is that censorship does not suppress all and only bad books, because its real intent is to suppress not *bad* books but *indecorous* books. *Lady Chatterley's Lover* "offends against decorum on a fairly gross scale. The problem . . . is that rules of decorum depend on social consensus" (304). In the absence of consensus, the only alternatives for the decorous are resignation or force. "The upholders of decorum must either impose their rule or else withdraw. There is no logic, no body of evidence by which decorum can plead for and justify itself." Milton shares with the prosecutors of *Lady Chatterley* the longing for a rational criterion by which to judge the worth of books, but Coetzee recognizes that what is at stake in censorship is not a rational, defensible criterion but a taboo. This recognition complicates the judgment on censorship. It means that the disagreement is not over whether the book is transgressive (both parties agree that it is), but over the nature and consequences of the transgression. "Once the tabooed representations have been brought into the light of day, does the taboo die, or is the slaying of the taboo to be acted out again and again, ritually? Does letting *Lady Chatterley* go free mean the beginning of the end of dirty books or the beginning of a stream of dirty books?" (313).

Coetzee agrees with Milton that censorship inhibits truth. Even beyond the obvious suppression of works after they are written, the threat of censorship exerts on writing some ugly, "deforming side effects that it is hard to escape." For instance, "the very fact that certain topics are forbidden creates an unnatural concentration upon them." But censorship may also, Coetzee suggests, invigorate truth. "Writing under the threat of official censure concentrates the mind wonderfully. I have no doubt that the intensity, the pointedness, the *seriousness* of Russian writing from the time of Nicholas I is in part a reflection of the fact that every word published represented a risk taken. *Mutatis mutandis,* I would say the same about much postwar writing from Eastern Europe" (299). Censorship cannot completely fail in its destructive intentions, but it cannot completely succeed.

Coetzee's own view about censorship "is what you would expect in any middle-class intellectual. I don't like censorship; where it exists, I would like to see it abolished; I think being a censor is an ignoble occupation" (298). But Coetzee refuses to be drawn unself-consciously into the paranoid, black-and-white, incorporative or expulsive "dynamic of stupidity" that has governed censorship debates. He does not permit his own view to become one-sided, acknowledging for instance that "I suspect it would be a pity if all boundaries were to disappear: in an abstract way I think there ought to be bounds to what is licit, if only as a way of making it possible to be transgressive." And he retains the ambition of rising above the stupidity of the debate, aiming instead "to say something intelligent about stupidity and the seeming inevitability of stupidity" (299).

Coetzee's argument against censorship is itself an act of censorship, but by facing up to the presence in his action of the activity it opposes, he at least avoids what Canetti calls "the moral kitsch of the Puritan": presenting oneself, even in self-accusation, as better than one is (106). Instead of abandoning "truth" and "freedom," as postmodern thinkers sometimes appear (even to themselves) to do, Coetzee has, by confronting their impurity, taken a step toward restoring two words we cannot allow to be completely consumed.

8 Postmodern Color

Ye white-lim'd walls! Ye alehouse painted signs!
Coal-black is better than another hue,
In that it scorns to bear another hue;
For all the water in the ocean
Can never turn the swan's black legs to white,
Although she lave them hourly in the flood.
           —*Shakespeare,* Titus Andronicus

His never having seen a photograph of a snow leopard in which the cat was not looking back at the camera leads the narrator in Prentiss Moore's poem "The Snow Leopard" to ask how often this white creature in a white landscape allows one "to see that it sees one," and to conclude that it "will never be taken by surprise." In the darkness that is our closest approximation to pure black, the darkness of an unlit alley or a forest on a starless night, we sense more than is there. Black is the color of unfettered imagination or (what is the same thing) unmitigated fear. Predators are born in the mind and released to snap twigs behind us with their paws, or crackle wind-blown week-old newspaper with their boots. Threat after threat hurtles across the edge of eyesight, as one fragment of the unconscious and then another seizes its chance to escape. But in the sunlit snow that is our closest natural approximation to pure white, the danger is blindness. We sense less than is there. In the snow one senses, in fact, hardly more than oneself: the movement of one's own shadow, the delicate crunch of the crust beneath one's feet at each step. At night we feel acutely the presence of the bear watching in the forest or the tough at the end of the alley, but in the day that sixth sense is oblivious to the leopard staring from the snow.

Jacques Derrida describes philosophy as snow-blind. Metaphysics, Derrida (de)claims, is "the white mythology which reassembles and reflects the culture of the West" (1982:213). In it, "the white man [mis]takes his own mythology, Indo-European mythology, his own *logos*, that is, the *mythos* of his idiom, for the universal form of that he must still wish to call Reason." Philosophy, Derrida says (in "White Mythology" as elsewhere) is a peculiar form of linguistic delusion, the mistaking of a private patois for the divine vox. But this linguistic error does not occur in isolation. Sins, like Ophelia's sorrows, come not single spies, and this Bonnie too has a Clyde. The same urge that leads us to mistake idiom for Word leads us to create a philosophical unconscious by repressing the origins of our concepts. "White mythology—metaphysics has erased within itself the fabulous scene that has produced it, the scene that nevertheless remains active and stirring, incribed in white ink, an invisible design covered over in the palimpsest." Like the Freudian psychical unconscious, the Derridean philosophical unconscious can never be fully repressed, but remains active and powerful through all attempts to eliminate it. Philosophy is, to borrow Antonio Porchia's words, the lamp we light at night so as not to see. It is whitewash that is never quite thick enough to hide what it covers. We shape our snow angels, oblivious to the leopard padding toward us.

Derrida thus expresses by a metaphor of color his discovery of the impurity in our ideas. But that only places him at the end of a long line. Nietzsche, for instance, isolates the impurity in that pervasive moral bromide, the concept of purity itself, warning his readers "against taking these concepts 'pure' and 'impure' too ponderously or broadly, not to say symbolically," because, as he puts it, "all the concepts of ancient man were rather at first incredibly uncouth, coarse, external, narrow, straightforward, and altogether unsymbolical in meaning to a degree that we can scarcely conceive" (1968c:467-68). The pure person, Nietzsche says, is simply the person who washes, "who forbids himself certain foods that produce skin ailments, who does not sleep with the dirty women of the lower strata." The pure person, in other words, is the one who prefers the light shades of cleanliness to the dark shades of the dirty, just as the concepts good and bad originate from a preference for light skin and hair over dark. For Nietzsche, the purity of the concept (the derivative metaphor) is contaminated by the concept of purity (the original metaphor). The concept "pure" itself can never be pure, forever tainted as it is by an origin that, like a birthmark, cannot be washed away.

Wittgenstein, too, beats Derrida to the punch. Near the beginning of the *Remarks on Colour*, he distinguishes between an ideal use of the word *white*, in which pure white is a rare but distinct form of white, and an ordinary use of *white* in which the question of purity does not arise. The ideal use of white purports to be a pure concept of the pure, but Wittgenstein points out that its permeation by the ordinary use of white makes even the ideal use inescapably impure:

> I, 3. Lichtenberg says that very few people have ever seen pure white. So do most people use the word wrong, then? And how did *he* learn the correct use?—He constructed an ideal use from the ordinary one. And that is not to say a better one, but one that has been refined along certain lines and in the process something has been carried to extremes.
> 4. And of course such a construct may in turn teach us something about the way we in fact use the word.
> 5. If I say a piece of paper is pure white, and if snow were placed next to it and it then appeared grey, in its normal surroundings I would still be right in calling it white and not light grey. It could be that I use a more refined concept of white in, say, a laboratory (where, for example, I also use a more refined concept of precise determination of time). (1978:2e)

I might be able to find (or create) a pigment such that a sample of that pigment would always appear whiter than a sample of any other pigment placed beside it, but a language game in which that pigment alone is white would function only within the attempt to find the pigment: it would have such a precise concept of white that only the inventors of the game could play it. The purity of purity (its refinement) is corrupted by an impurity (its being carried to extremes) from which it cannot be separated.

William Gass monitors in a chromatic hue the same footage Nietzsche and Wittgenstein screened in black and white. With the application of a little blush, the cheeks of even a celluloid Scarlett can be red, but purity is always already gone with the wind. Rather than being (pure) embodiments of the rationality and volition of thinking subjects, concepts, according to Gass, settle onto words the way dust settles onto furniture. "A random set of meanings has softly gathered around the word the way lint collects. . . . We cover our concepts, like fish, with clouds of net" (7).

Like the air Anaximenes advertises as the *archē*, meaning is all around us: we breathe it in, and like Anaximenes' air, it condenses into concepts by a process of felting. Unlike Freud, for whom the apparently random melange of a complex is actually infused with order and thus is susceptible to purification by the analyst, for Gass, the apparent orderliness of a word/concept like "blue" (which must be orderly because we know how to use it) is actually infused with disorder, and thus is inherently, incurably impure. Instead of being assembled by that gentle giant, the jeweler-God of the argument from design, a concept gets trampled into existence by the clumsiness of circumstance. "So *blue*, the word and the condition, the color and the act, contrive to contain one another, as if the bottle of the genii were its belly, the lamp's breath the smoke of the wraith" (11). Blue "is the color of the mind in borrow of the body" (57), and thus a proof that Descartes was wrong about the purity of the mind. If blue is "the color of interior life" (76), it is also the color of death (11); blue may be "the godlike hue" (69), but that makes it no less true that "Being without Being is blue" (12).

Other philosophers have beaten Derrida to the punch, but philosophers do not have a corner on the market of color as a sign of conceptual impurity. If philosophers have used color as a tool for discovering hidden impurity, it is not because they have found in color the impurity its naive artistic practitioners have ignored. Van Gogh speaks in his later letters, for instance, about chromatic hues as the "endless varieties of grays," consisting always of an admixture of black and white with the "fundamental colors" or the "composites." And Joseph Albers shows ad nauseum in his *Interaction of Color* that no color is pure, uninfluenced by the color(s) to which it is adjacent.

The interest of "White Mythology," then, lies not in the simple (re)discovery of impurity by a color metaphor, but in Derrida's description of the nature of that impurity. His color metaphor, white mythology, is a metaphor for metaphor, and so enacts in particular form the simultaneously autogenic and autophagic character he attributes to metaphor in general. It initiates a sequence of metaphors that generate and then consume each other. The impurity to which Derrida is snow-blind is the persistence, through his sequence of metaphors, of two other metaphors he does not notice, but which, although they are necessary for his own view, also entail the view he opposes.

Philosophy tries to fit metaphor into a teleology of truth by a noble lie: metaphor is a road that leads from concept to truth. But

Derrida argues that metaphor has neither beginning nor end, and so leads only from itself to itself. In imitation of his more famous maxim that there is nothing outside the text, Derrida claims in "White Mythology" that there is nothing outside metaphor. Concepts do not precede metaphor, and truth does not follow after metaphor. By the standard postmodern strategy of reframing the discussion of metaphor as a discussion of space rather than as a discussion of time, Derrida makes metaphor a matter of structure rather than design.

Modernist views typically assign metaphor the characteristics that Christianity assigned to memory. Metaphor becomes, as memory was for Augustine in the *Confessions*, the function that can overcome the absence of past and future, can make them present as past and future are continuously present to God, who is timeless and eternal. But that is a diachronic view, in which issues of meaning distribute themselves over time, in which presence and absence are temporal. In keeping with the preference for synchronic views characteristic of postmodern theorists, Derrida changes the question of metaphor from present, past, and future to inside and outside.

His first expression of a thesis thus consists of transforming temporal terms (etymology) into spatial terms (covering, containing). The primitive meaning of a word is sensory and material, but does not become a metaphor until "philosophical discourse puts it into circulation. Simultaneously the first meaning and the first displacement are then forgotten. The metaphor is no longer noticed, and it is taken for the proper meaning" (1982:211). That diachrony matters, though, only because it results in a synchronic state: "abstract notions always hide a sensory figure" (210), the same figure painted in white and covered over in white that becomes a restless palimpsest.

Through such metaphors for metaphor as the sun, from which he concludes that the "metaphorization of metaphor, its bottomless overdeterminability," is "inscribed in the structure of metaphor" and reveals its "multiple, divided origin" (243-44), Derrida continues his spatial figures until he arrives at the conclusion that, because metaphor is irreducibly plural and ungoverned by a "central" metaphor, it "gets carried away with itself" and "cannot be what it is except in erasing itself, indefinitely constructing its own destruction" (268). Therefore the consumption of metaphysics by metaphor is "presence disappearing in its own radiance, the hidden source of light, of truth, and of meaning, the erasure of the visage of Being."

If Derrida is right about the ubiquity of metaphor, and the consequent creation of an unconscious in texts, then his own text can hardly hope to erase the stirrings of the "invisible design" that is "inscribed in white ink" on the palimpsest of his own white mythology. The concepts I have named the "constitutive other" and the "alien other" are the lemon juice that can raise the white ink on Derrida's page.

Humans incessantly search for themselves in what is not themselves, a fact that goes a long way toward explaining our fascination with mirrors and photographs and home videos, as well as the feeling Freud describes as "uncanny," brought on by the experience of "the double": all these captivate because, although we usually *fail* to find ourselves in the other, in them we actually *succeed*. Postmodern theorists, who talk of "alterity," "otherness," and "difference" as frequently as did the existentialists of "authenticity," make this search central to their ideas.

The terms describing the object of the search may be new, but not the search itself. Nietzsche, for example, begins his brief meditation on translations in *The Gay Science* with the pronouncement that "the degree of the historical sense of any age may be inferred from the manner in which this age makes translations and tries to absorb former ages and books" (1974:136-37). He goes on to praise the seventeenth- and eighteenth-century French for taking "possession of Roman antiquity in a way for which we would no longer have courage enough," and the Romans for having done the same with Greek antiquity. The Romans "took hold of everything good and lofty of Greek antiquity," Nietzsche says. "How they translated things into the Roman present! How deliberately and recklessly they brushed the dust off the wings of the butterfly that is called moment!" (137). For Nietzsche absorption is the important point, and his argument does not advocate, but opposes "historical sense." We should, he says, "make new for ourselves what is old and find ourselves in it."

Even while he is attempting to question one assumption, though, Nietzsche makes another: he assumes that we find ourselves in the old—that is, in a temporal continuum. Recent movements that call themselves "postmodern," though, question that assumption, too, by trying to find ourselves not in the old but in the distant—that is, in a spatial continuum.

No matter what the group in which one claims membership, that group has both spatial and temporal boundaries. Take the group of United States citizens. The spatial boundaries are fairly clearly the geographical borders of the country. Even though there are exceptions like resident aliens, the exceptions themselves confirm the meaningfulness of the boundaries: crossing one of the boundaries without permission of the group justifies punishment by the group. The temporal boundaries are 1776 in one direction and the future in the other. Neither Native Americans nor colonists living in what would become the United States were U. S. citizens in 1775, and the children who will be born to U.S. citizens five years from now are not yet U.S. citizens, even though they will be.

Outside these spatial and temporal boundaries lurks the Other. The Other can make one what one is, or it can threaten to destroy what one is. That Other which makes one what one is, I call "constitutive." The Other which threatens what one is, I call "alien." Modernism saw the constitutive Other as distributed over time, and the alien Other as distributed over space: in other words, we are separated by temporal boundaries from the Other that makes us ourselves, and by spatial boundaries from the Other that threatens to destroy our identity. History liberates, the foreign threatens. The U.S. typifies this view: it sees its identity as constituted by its historical origins in the pilgrims, the "founding fathers," and so on. What preceded us makes us what we are. Our identity is threatened by such phenomena as communism, which is contemporary but which threatens to contaminate from the outside. Postmodernism, reversing the modernist view, sees the constitutive Other as distributed over space, and the alien Other as distributed over time. The external liberates, tradition threatens. Modernism is xenophobic, and postmodernism mnemophobic.

Modernism sought the constitutive other in time and the alien other in space because its roots were in Judaism and Christianity. (This is true even when it is rebelling against them, as shown by the frequency with which aging moderns like Eliot and Auden fell back into Christianity.) Centuries of diaspora dictated that Judeochristianity find itself in time: it could not find itself in space when it had no space. Temporal connection was all that was left to it, so it talked always of the past, when the patriarchs spoke with God and conquered their enemies, and the future, when the Messiah would come and the sheep be separated from the goats. Postmodernism seeks the constitutive other in space and the alien other in time because its roots are in paganism. We need not long for a future in which we shall know even as also we are known, or a past when our ancestors walked with the Lord God in the garden in the cool of the day, if the gods are everywhere.

This change between where "modernism" and "postmodernism" seek the constitutive other appears nowhere more clearly than in the continuing clamor over college core curriculum. A comparison between two documents like Lynne Cheney's *50 Hours: A Core Curriculum for College Students* and Henry Louis Gates's *Loose Canons: Notes on the Culture Wars* shows that advocates of the "great books" and advocates of "multiculturalism" divide very neatly along this temporal vs. spatial distinction. Even such relatively balanced and nontendentious books as these cannot help but reveal their orientation, and they do so even in the process of accommodating the opposite viewpoint.

Cheney's temporal preference emerges clearly not only in her recommendations but in the justifications she gives for them. For instance, in explaining why study of "Cultures and Civilizations" matters, she says it "provides students opportunities to explore the *formative periods* of civilization on several continents; to follow the *development* of Western society and thought; . . . and to understand as well the *evolution* of other traditions" (19; my italics). Her explanation for requiring study of two non-Western civilizations is also temporal: such study follows an intellectual tradition, and exemplifies values "long characteristic of the West" (24). Just as Cheney incorporates understanding of the world into the temporal metaphors of origin, evolution, and tradition, so Gates incorporates understanding of history into spatial metaphors of vision, decentering, and marginality, as in this passage:

> Americans know so very little about world history and culture in part because high school and college core curricula, in this country, center upon European and American societies, with America represented as the logical conclusion or summary of civilization since the Greeks, in the same way that Christians believe that Christ is the culmination of the Old Testament prophets. Our ignorance of physical geography is a symptom of a much broader ignorance of the world's cultural geography. (112-13)

The distinction between the "constitutive Other" and the "alien Other" explains the consistency with which "great books" advocates like Cheney formulate their justifications in temporal terms and "multiculturalism" advocates like Gates formulate theirs in spatial terms. Great books advocates consistently use temporal justifications because they see the constitutive other distributed over time and the alien other distributed over space. Multiculturalists consistently use spatial justifications because they see the constitutive other distributed over space and the alien other distributed over time.

The distinction between the constitutive other and the alien other may reveal itself most clearly in the "culture wars," but it inhabits many other differences between modern and postmodern theory, like the preoccupation with neurosis in the one and with schizophrenia in the other. Freud devotes himself almost exclusively to neurosis, which he treats as a temporal disorientation. The problem, he says, is a discontinuity between the patient's past self or selves and his or her present self. The analyst must discover in the discourse of the patient all the parts of a coherent narrative, upon rearrangement of which into an Aristotelian mythos with beginning, middle, and end the patient will be cured. Thus Freud uses the archeologist as his totem for the analyst. Freud admits that his technique, so successful, he claims, in healing neuroses, cannot help victims of psychoses, including schizophrenics. He couches his explanation of that inability in terms of transference, but postmoderns like Deleuze and Guattari explain it as the inability of a temporal treatment to deal with a spatial problem.

Deleuze and Guattari deny Freud's distinction between neuroses and psychoses: "between neurosis and psychosis there is no difference in nature, species, or group" (1983:130). That enables them to reduce all mental illness to the single illness of schizophrenia, making it "our very own 'malady,' [post]modern man's sickness." But if neurosis for Freud is a temporal disorientation, schizophrenia for Deleuze and Guattari is a spatial disorientation. The Freudian neurotic does not know the difference between now and then; the postmodern schizophrenic does not know the difference between here and there.

The schizo knows how to leave: he has made departure into something as simple as being born or dying. But at the same time his journey is strangely stationary, in place. He does not speak of another world, he is not from another world: even when he is displacing himself in space, his is a journey in intensity, around the desiring-machine that is erected here and remains here. (131)

If neurosis is the modern madness, schizophrenia is the postmodern madness.

The change from a constitutive other in time to a constitutive other in space has political consequences as well. When the constitutive other was temporal, the object of war was destruction / mastery of the alien other, that which threatens one's past or future from outside. Civil war, war with others who share one's space, alone could not be justified, and was, as Hobbes makes clear, to be avoided at all costs. Its perpetrators had to describe it as "revolution," or in other words as war against those who only appear to share our space but really threaten to take away our future. When the constitutive other is spatial, as it must be in a "global village," any war is a civil war. "There is," says Baudrillard, "no more space for war" (1990:14). Destruction of the alien other can occur only by the uniquely postmodern, because media-dependent, activity of terrorism, which, as Baudrillard points out, "has no revolutionary consequences" (1983:51), and so aims not at preserving but destroying the future, which it accomplishes by its unpredictability. This removal of the future is the meaning of an act such as hostage-taking: by making the outcome incalculable and arbitrary, the hostage-takers steal the future from the hostage and the group from whom the hostage was taken.

The threats of war are spatial, of terrorism temporal, so no longer does the outside threaten us as alienation, but the future threatens us as terror: "We are all hostages, and we are all terrorists. This circuit has replaced that other one of masters and slaves, the dominating and the dominated, the exploiters and the exploited. Gone is the constellation of the slave and the proletarian: from now on it is the hostage and the terrorist. Gone is the constellation of alienation; from now on it is that of terror" (1990:39).

Even the reversal of the identity / difference hierarchy from modernism to postmodernism can be explained by the distinction between constitutive and alien other. Both modernism and postmodernism privilege the constitutive other, but they connect different terms with it. Modernism links identity to the constitutive other, because it characterizes identity as that which is continuous over a span of time. Postmodernism links difference to the constitutive other, because it sees difference as that which is distributed over space. For modernism, identity generates meaning; for postmodernism, difference generates meaning. The two views share belief in the constitutive other as the origin (in modernism) or the site (in postmodernism) of meaning. Moderns and postmoderns agree on valorization of the constitutive other over the alien other, but a whole series of their conflicts can be traced to disagreement over how the other is distributed over space and time.

Racism is one cultural phenomenon in which the metaphor of color reveals its connection to concepts of purity, and the change from racism to "multiculturalism" is one way in which postmodernism has begun to construe the constitutive other as distributed not across time but across space, and the alien other as distributed not across space but across time. Anglo-European society (or part of it) has begun learning to construe other races (those spatially but not temporally distinct from it) as constitutive others rather than as alien others. One need cite neither a long list of racists among the intellectual parents of modernism (Kant, Darwin, and others) nor a long list of the historical effluvia of racism (the Crusades, slavery in the American South, and the like), to make the point that other races were for centuries considered alien others by the hegemonic culture in Europe and America. In the context of a discussion of color, the single example of Goethe's *Theory of Colours* will be illustration enough.

Goethe is not a Hitler or George Wallace of the intellect, but even his apparently innocuous aesthetic theory is marred by a racist discoloration. He is confident that color reveals character: "that the colour of the skin and hair has relation with the differences of character, is beyond question" (265). We all know, do we not, that red hair is a sign of lubriciousness in women, and dark hair a sign of aggressiveness in men? His explicit claim takes an aesthetic form: "we venture . . . to assert that the white man, that is, he whose surface varies from white to reddish, yellowish, brownish, in short, whose surface appears most neutral in hue and least inclines to any particular or positive colour, is the most beautiful." This claim about the beauty of humans follows from a general claim, made much earlier in the book, about the beauty of colors. "Every decided colour," Goethe says, "does a certain violence to the eye, and forces the organ to opposition" (25). Still, it demands no great subtlety of thought to see the connection between racism presented as an aesthetic view and its explicitly political form.

This type of view, in which white is the one pure hue, is of course exactly the type of view against which Derrida's idea of a "white mythology" is directed. But in "White Mythology" a modernist ghost haunts the postmodern machine. It should surprise no one that a text that denies the purity of purity will not itself be pure. A text that removes the mote from its brother's eye will have a beam in its own, and a text that spies the bear stalking its sister will not see the snow leopard stalking it. I am not by this sequence of observations hinting at an accusation of racism in Derrida. I mean neither to call up images of white-cloaked klansmen nor to tar Derrida with the same brush used on DeMan. I do mean to assert, though, that in "White Mythology" Derrida is not able to treat the alien other as distributed exclusively over time and the constitutive other exclusively over space. The very act of denying the legitimacy of the white/pure metaphor will depend on using the aspects of the white/pure metaphor that ground racism.

The color/word/concept "white" has several qualities not shared by other hues, two of which are relevant here. Wittgenstein returns again and again in his *Remarks on Colour* to the theme that white alone of all the colors cannot be transparent. But the force of the "cannot" is logical, not empirical. "The question is: is constructing a 'transparent white body' like constructing a 'regular biangle'?" (35e). Wittgenstein's observation seems unrelated to racism (even though its stimulus is Goethe's *Theory of Colours*) until it is juxtaposed with the first paragraph of Ralph Ellison's novel:

> I am an invisible man. No, I am not a spook like those who haunted Edgar Allan Poe; nor am I one of your Hollywood-movie ectoplasms. I am a man of substance, of flesh and bone, fiber and liquids—and I might even be said to possess a mind. I am invisible, understand, simply because people refuse to see me. Like the bodiless heads you see sometimes in circus sideshows, it is as though I have been surrounded by mirrors of hard, distorting glass. When they approach me they see only my surroundings, themselves, or figments of their imagination—indeed, everything and anything except me. (3)

White is the one color that, although it can render other colors invisible, cannot itself become (or be made) invisible.

Wittgenstein reveals the conceptual corollary when he connects the concept of transparency to the concept of depth. "Why is it that something can be transparent green but not transparent white?

Transparency and reflections exist only in the dimension of depth of a visual image. The impression that a transparent medium makes is that something lies behind the medium" (5e). It is possible to paint a transparent red body, but if you substitute white for red, "you no longer have the impression of transparency; just as you no longer have the impression of solidity if you turn this drawing ▱ into this one ▭" (19e). If white is substituted for a red that was merely surface, the surface automatically acquires depth. White as a mere surface without depth is logically impossible:

146. A body that is actually transparent can, of course, seem white to us; but it cannot seem white and transparent.
147. But we should not express this by saying: white is not a transparent colour.
149. An element of visual space may be white or red, but can't be either transparent or opaque.
150. Transparency and reflection only exist in the dimension of depth of a visual image.

We cannot even *think* of white without depth: "we cannot describe (e.g. paint), how something white and clear would look, and that means: we don't know what description, portrayal, these words demand of us" (5e). In other words, white is not only the one hue that can never be transparent; it is so *because* it is the one hue that can never be merely surface, but must have depth. Red or black can exist as the mere surface of an image whose other colors have depth, but white must always itself have depth.

The metaphor of purity in romanticism and modernism for which white has been the vehicle has had as its tenors, then, opacity and depth. Derrida attempts in "White Mythology" to deconstruct that metaphor by changing from a diachronic to a synchronic view. But he does not, and cannot, entirely succeed. Diachrony permeates synchrony no less than synchrony permeates diachrony. Jan Zwicky says that "few words are capsized on the surface of language, subject to every redefining breeze. Most, though they have drifted, are nonetheless anchored, their meanings holding out for centuries against the sweep of rationalist desire" (166). Derrida cannot capsize the concept(s) associated with the word "white."

In the "Exergue," Derrida makes his plan explicit. Criticizing the view of metaphor in Anatole France's *The Garden of Epicurus*, Derrida says, "to read within a concept the hidden history of a metaphor is to privilege *diachrony* at the expense of system," to define metaphor as the resemblance between two signs, and to assume "semantic 'depth'" (1982:215). Derrida's own view will be very different: "it goes without saying that far from belonging to this problematic and sharing its presuppositions, the question of metaphor, such as we are repeating it here, on the contrary should delimit them." Derrida will replace the "continuist presupposition," according to which metaphor is depicted in temporal terms as "a progressive erosion" or "an uninterrupted exhausting of the primitive meaning," with a view of metaphor in spatial terms as "a displacement with breaks" or "separations without origin."

In doing so, however, Derrida will use the metaphors of opacity and depth that ground the very view he is opposing. In "Plus de métaphore," he shows why a systematic treatise on metaphor is impossible. But his conclusion depends on the language of opacity and depth. "The general taxonomy of metaphors . . . would presuppose the solution" of the problems that constitute philosophy (228). But "presuppose" (like other verbs in this paragraph, such as "constitute" and "base") is a word in which the metaphor goes unnoticed, and the metaphor (from the Latin *sub-* and *ponere*) is one of depth: placing under. Opacity enters when he says that philosophy "could perceive its metaphorics only around a blind spot," the contour of which metaphor would describe. So while philosophy (or part of it) can be invisible, a blind spot, metaphor cannot.

In the next section, "The Ellipsis of the Sun," examining Aristotle's view of metaphor, Derrida shows Aristotle at work relegating metaphor to "ancillary status" in the service of the "discourse of full truth" (238), but he identifies as a slip Aristotle's incidental invocation of "the case of a *lexis* that would be metaphorical in all its aspects" (243). In his discussion of that slip, though, Derrida himself slips both opacity and depth in through the back door. Depth is integral to metaphor in the form of bottomlessness, an endless overdeterminability "inscribed in the structure of metaphor." Opacity, too, is integral. Once the metaphorical relation starts, "the punctual source of truth or properness" becomes invisible, a star overwhelmed by the sun of metaphor. Metaphor announces "the multiple, divided origin of all seed, of the eye, of invisibility, death, the father, the 'proper name,' etc." (244). Metaphor is that which alone cannot be transparent or invisible, even when it renders invisible all else.

In "The Flowers of Rhetoric," Derrida claims that no philosophy has ever renounced the Aristotelian ideal of univocity in language, and then argues (as he has argued elsewhere) that philosophy should renounce that ideal in favor of a "nonmasterable dissemination." The Aristotelian view of metaphor is "unceasingly, unwillingly" drawn to or turned toward the sun as guarantor of univocity, but Derrida argues that the sun is a source of dissemination instead. The pattern, though, matches the pattern in the preceding sections: Derrida's argument depends on and privileges opacity and depth. Although the sun itself can disappear, it does so only by keeping out of sight, not by becoming transparent. Yet it conditions the possibility of invisibility: "the very opposition of appearing and disappearing, the entire lexicon of the *phainesthai*, of *aletheia*, etc., of day and night, of the visible and the invisible, of the present and the absent—all this is possible only under the sun" (251). The sun, like the color white, cannot be transparent. Similarly, once metaphor turns toward the sun, depth is necessary: "this abyss of metaphor will never cease to stratify itself" (253).

The same pattern recurs in the final section, "*La méta-physique—relève de la métaphore.*" Derrida begins by stating the conclusion at which the preceding sections arrive: "metaphor is less in the philosophical text (and in the rhetorical text coordinated with it) than the philosophical text is within metaphor" (258). He then asks about the possibility of a meta-metaphorics. Predictably, though, his answer to that question depends on opacity and depth. Because metaphor is "plural from the outset," it generates "a text which is not exhausted in the history of its meaning . . . , in the visible or invisible presence of its theme" (268). The metaphoric text is never itself invisible, though it can occasion invisibility. It is also necessarily deep. In the traditional view, its return to itself is an interiorization, and interiorization is possible only for an entity with depth, not for an entity that has only surface. In the Derridean view, the repetition of the metaphoric text takes the form not of an endless return to itself, but of endlessly putting itself into the abyss, or in other words into infinite depth.

Derrida knew in advance that his project had to fail. He says that "a metaphorology would be derivative as concerns the discourse it allegedly would dominate, whether it does so by taking as its rule the explicit consciousness of the philosopher or the systematic and objective structure of his text" (228). One cannot "dominate philosophical metaphorics." Even a philosophy that describes philosophy as snow-blind is philosophy, so it will be as snow-blind as the rest. What he did not know was *how* his project would fail. Derrida knew that "there is a code or a program—a rhetoric, if you will—for every discourse on metaphor" (231). What he did not know was that even in a discourse deconstructing "white mythology," the code or program of his discourse would depend on the very features of the concept of white, opacity and depth, most important to the negative phenomena like racism that grow out of white mythology.

9   Postmodern Love

O, learn to read what silent love hath writ.
—Shakespeare, Sonnet 23

As the title of Raymond Carver's short story implies, "what we talk about when we talk about love" is always something other than love. When movies and romance novels talk about love, they talk about sex, and when self-help books talk about love they talk about overcoming chemical dependency, learning to risk rejection, or healing the emotional scars of childhood. Nowhere is Hegel's maxim that "we meant something other than we meant to mean" more true than in discourse about love. If we can ever mean what we say, we cannot do so when we say we love. Like a photograph in certain tribal cultures, a declaration of love steals a soul, and like mimetic art in Plato, discourse about love only diminishes its object. Love transcends discourse, so that to declare love signifies that one does not possess it. As discourse about God cannot teach us about God, so discourse about love cannot teach us about love.

Still, postmodern theorists, for whom all is discourse (and for whom, therefore, nothing, including love, can transcend discourse), talk about love, so even one who does not expect to learn about love through discourse might engage in discourse about love to learn about postmodernism.

Love shares with the sign a morphology and a teleology. Love has always been depicted as a sphere (the geometrical symbol for completion and wholeness), and no example of such a depiction is more delightful than Aristophanes' speech in the *Symposium*, in which the gods avenge themselves on humans for the mortals' attempt to "scale the heights of heaven and set upon the gods" by splitting the humans in half, from their former globular, eight-limbed shape into our current form: two arms, two legs, and (alas) only one set of genitals. This divine division was the origin of absence and desire, leaving "each half with a desperate yearning for the other," so that "they ran together and flung their arms around each other's necks, and asked for nothing better than to be rolled into one" (Plato 191a). More than twenty centuries later, Saussure gives the sign a strikingly similar shape, depicting the signifier and the signified as two hemispheres that unite to form the sign. Signifier and signified are so "intimately united" that, not only does "each recall the other" (66), but indeed they do not exist independently. As for their aim, love and the sign both pursue unity. Offered the opportunity by Hephæstus to be welded together so strongly that even in the next world they would be inseparable, "no lover on earth," Aristophanes says, "would dream of refusing." So inseparable are the sign's parts, says Saussure, that it resembles a sheet of paper, whose two sides are the signifier and the signified: "one cannot cut the front without cutting the back at the same time" (113).

Given such similarities, when postmodern thinkers, preoccupied as they are with language, use language to talk about love, they surprise no one by identifying language and love each with the other. Both Julia Kristeva, in *Tales of Love*, and Roland Barthes, in *A Lover's Discourse*, make exactly that identification, but they do so subversively, under cover of an apparently contradictory claim, denying to love the "structurality" that each considers a characteristic feature of language, so that love no longer has a code for Kristeva or a system for Barthes.

When Kristeva laments that "we lack a code of love," adding that we have "no stable mirrors for the loves of a period, group, or class" (1980:6), she is right in the sense that the result of any attempt to produce an *Ars amatoria* or *De Amore* for our time would be as absurd as Ovid's and Andreas's works themselves are. It would be not only hopelessly naive, but meaningless, to try to specify like Andreas the number of persons to whom "love can legitimately be revealed" or to enumerate "what things lovers can properly accept when partners offer gifts." But Kristeva asks not whether a code of love exists, but what sort of code it is and how well it functions. She means not that in contemporary society no code of love exists, but that the code that does exist is failing. We lack a code of love not in the sense that we do not have one, but in the sense that the one we do have is lacking. "The conclusion of the twentieth century," she says, "hands down to us an unbearable amorous space" (124). Like Kristeva, Barthes asserts the disappearance of a code of love:

"today," he says, "there is no system of love" (1978:211). And like Kristeva, Barthes means not that the code does not exist, but that it is failing: "whether he seeks to prove his love, or to discover if the other loves him, the amorous subject has no system of sure signs at his disposal" (214).

When two postmodern theorists agree that love once was encoded but is encoded no longer, we should suspect that they mean something other than they meant to mean, since if we have learned anything from postmodern theory, we have learned that phenomena always have codes. Molly Peacock's description of love as "the structure we determine / to live in" captures the necessity of love's being encoded, but even without that necessity we would know to look for some other meaning when two believers in the ubiquity of structure deny a structure to love.

That other meaning is not merely the equation of love and language, to which each readily admits, and which neither has any motive for repressing. Barthes reveals his equation of love and language when he says that, because "signs are not proofs," one "falls back, paradoxically, on the omnipotence of language" (215). There is no code of love distinct from other codes, because love is code. As easily as one slips from pantheism to atheism (if nothing is not God, nothing is God), Barthes slips from love's having no code to love's having only code. Barthes wants love to be, like all else for a semiologist, language. For the lover, according to Barthes, everything signifies: everything "is received not as a fact but in the aspect of a sign which must be interpreted" (63). The lover, as represented in this case by Goethe's Werther, "creates meaning, always and everywhere, out of nothing, and it is meaning which thrills him: he is in the crucible of meaning" (67). Remember Freud's appeal, when he wants to prove that every mental phenomenon signifies, to the fact that lovers know to interpret everything, even "a glance, scarcely noticed by other people," as meaningful. Kristeva reveals her equation of love and language when she talks of "the infinity of the signifier" as "the only *infinite* space where we might unfurl our loves."

The meaning repressed by Barthes' and Kristeva's denial of structurality to love is not the equation of love and language, but that love is for them a transcendental signified. They are motivated to repress that meaning because to admit the existence of a transcendental signified would be to admit that language is not only an explanans but also an explanandum; that in other words, even if structure gives meaning, it is also given meaning by something that escapes it. Love's position as a transcendental signified is revealed by Barthes' and Kristeva's attempt to attribute to it two apparently contradictory properties: inexpressibility and omnisignificance. Love, in other words, like language, can neither be put into words, nor fail to signify. Because, as Kristeva puts it, "there is no act . . . outside of love" (274), as there is nothing outside the text for Derrida, love cannot be expressed in language, nor can language be anything but love. Barthes and Kristeva on love reveal the desire of postmodern theory in general to make language into the map that, like the one in Borges's parable, becomes the territory.

The problem is that love cannot be expressed, cannot be put into language, any more than can God or nature or the good or any other transcendental signified. Love will not be mastered by language, and in the final analysis neither Kristeva nor Barthes manages to deny this. Kristeva acknowledges in her book's third sentence that "the language of love is impossible" (1). Barthes has to admit that "*I-love-you* has no usages" (148). He says, "*I-love-you* is not a sentence: it does not transmit a meaning." Or, even more explicitly, "*I-love-you* belongs neither in the realm of linguistics nor in that of semiology."

Barthes and Kristeva equate love's inexpressibility and omnisignificance, because each of those conditions differs from love's being (or having) *a* code. Love can meet those conditions only if it is not *a* structure, but *structure*. If love exceeds language but subsumes it, as by definition transcendental signifieds do, then it will be both inexpressible and omnisignificant. Love is the uncanny double of signification, able to transfer "mental processes from the one person to the other—what we should call telepathy—so that the one possesses knowledge, feeling and experience in common with the other," but in which at the same time the "self becomes confounded, or the foreign self is substituted" for it (Freud 1950:387). If for signification difference discloses identity, for love identity discloses difference.

Postmodern theorists have been as naive in their belief that an account of language will reveal meaning as was Russell in his belief that an account of logic would reveal truth. We need a modern-day Wittgenstein who can return postmodern theory's repressed knowledge that what structures language is outside language, just as the *Tractatus* returned Russell's repressed knowledge that what structures logic is outside logic.

Postmodern theory has not been able to "decenter" love, to unseat it from the transcendent position it occupies in Plato and

Christianity and all the derivative religio-philosophical discourses of the west. Love remains a limit of discourse, a *rature* everything is *sous*. Nowhere is this relation between love and language better dramatized than in *Anna Karenina* when Kitty and Levin declare their love to each other by writing, in chalk on a table while a party is going on around them, only the initial letters of the words in a long conversation. Levin writes, "*w, y, g, m, t, a, i, i, n, p, d, y, m, i, w, n, b, p, o, t, i, w, p, t ?,*" and Kitty blushes because she understands it. She writes a series of initials that he understands, and so on, until this resolution: "He could not fill in the words she meant at all, but in her lovely eyes, radiant with happiness, he understood everything he had to know. He wrote down three letters; but before he had even finished writing she had already read it under his hand; she had finished it herself, and written down the answer: 'Yes'" (Tolstoy 425).

Kitty and Levin did not need to communicate, because they were one. They did not need language, because they *were* language. Where each interlocutor is what the other wants to say, speech is obsolete. Love remains the discursive ideal: a language that erases itself by becoming language, that no longer needs to signify because it is signification itself, the resolution of two (signifier, signified) into one (sign). The Derridean "infinite play of substitutions" ends when meaning is replaced by identity.

Like the rest of us, Kristeva and Barthes talk not *about* love but *around* it, because in postmodernism, as in any other argot, "love" names the transcendental signified, the transparent mingling of truth, desire, and presence, that which even when it is nothing is everything.

10   Postmodern Sex

. . . ever as she could with haste dispatch
She'd come again, and with a greedy ear
Devour up my discourse.
                    —*Shakespeare*, Othello

When Jim, the man in Nicholson Baker's *Vox*, says to Abby, the woman, "I *love* the telephone," she expresses no surprise at a statement that, in the middle of a conversation enumerating the sexual idiosyncracies of its interlocutors, could be taken in any number of perverse ways. She even (without hesitation) seconds his view: "'Well, I like it too,' she said. 'There's a power it has'" (58). Later she expands on the point: "Sometimes I think with the telephone that if I concentrate enough I could pour myself into it and I'd be turned into a mist and I would rematerialize in the room of the person I'm talking to" (95). Nothing could be less surprising today than a "thing" for telephones, except perhaps that an imagined dialogue between two fictitious persons a continent apart recounting imaginary sex could become a bestseller, or be described by the review quoted on the front cover as "breathtaking." Like Bastidides in Ezra Pound's "The Temperaments," our age "both talks and writes of nothing save copulation," even though like Bastidides we no longer practice what we preach. To rings far enough from the magnet, almost anything counts as attraction.

Had Michel Foucault lived to read Baker's novel, he would have construed *Vox* not as an isolated phenomenon, but as one result of a centuries-long attempt, begun by the Greeks and continued by Christianity, to transform sex into discourse. Foucault devotes his three-volume *History of Sexuality* to an argument against a widely held view of sexuality, a view he labels "the repressive hypothesis." According to that hypothesis, contemporary sexual ideas and behavior can best be understood as the result of repression initially performed on Greek and Roman sexual license by early Christians, and reimposed on the temporary sexual liberalism of the Renaissance by the prudish Victorians. Even Freud could only alter but not escape this repressive history: "if repression has indeed been the fundamental link between power, knowledge, and sexuality since the classical age," Foucault says, "it stands to reason that we will not be able to free ourselves from it except at a considerable cost: nothing less than a transgression of laws, a lifting of prohibitions, an irruption of speech, a reinstating of pleasure within reality, and a whole new economy in the mechanisms of power will be required" (1990a:5). Freud was too "circumspect," "prudent," and "innocuous" to escape this repression: "one cannot hope to obtain the desired results simply from a medical practice, nor from a theoretical discourse, however rigorously pursued."

The psychological advantages offered by the repressive hypothesis to its proponents lead Foucault to distrust it. The repressive hypothesis allows its adherents to project onto Christianity blame for the initial wave of repression and onto capitalism blame for the second, and allows those same adherents to portray themselves as Promethean heroes: "if sex is repressed, that is, condemned to prohibition, nonexistence, and silence, then the mere fact that one is speaking about it has the appearance of a deliberate transgression" (6).

The repressive hypothesis claims that Christianity and capitalism repressed the ability of the Greeks and renaissance Europeans to talk about and engage in sex freely, and in place of that freedom substituted silence and celibacy. Foucault argues that in fact the projects of the allegedly opposed traditions are continuous, and that the result of each is the opposite of silence. Instead of a picture according to which the Greeks could fuck and talk about it, but Christians could do neither, Foucault paints a picture according to which Greeks and Christians, renaissance citizens and capitalists, all try to transform fucking into talking, and in which in this postmodern age we have begun to "succeed" in that transformation.

Christianity, on Foucault's view, *did* want to prevent sex from talking, but instead of trying to silence sex, Christianity chose the other means to that end: to make sex *become* talk. Discourse cannot speak, it can only be spoken. So Christianity adopted the same strategy as the Greeks: to dominate sex by making it passive and therefore neutralizing it. Instead of choosing, like many Oriental cultures, "initiation and the masterful secret" as the discursive form of sex, Christianity chose as its discursive form confession. Instead of letting sex retain its own power, Christianity distributed that power among humans, in a "rich get richer" pattern, so that wherever confession is not voluntarily performed it can, because of the uneven distribution of power, be "wrung from a person by violence or threat" (59), making torture confession's shadow. Confession is, after all, "a ritual that unfolds within a power relationship, for one does not confess without the presence (or virtual presence) of a partner who is not simply the interlocutor but the authority who requires the confession, prescribes and appreciates it, and intervenes in order to judge, punish, forgive, console, and reconcile" (61-62).

Confession became scientific discourse on sexuality after "the obtaining of the confession and its effects were recodified as therapeutic operations" by people like Charcot and Freud (67). The Christian imperative regarding sexuality was to "transform your desire, your every desire, into discourse," or in other words to pass "everything having to do with sex through the endless mill of speech" (21). Although Christianity failed, its sexual imperative, according to Foucault, worked all too well. In our era, "sex, the revelation of truth, the overturning of global laws, the proclamation of a new day to come, and the promise of a certain felicity are linked together. Today it is sex that serves as a support for the ancient form—so familiar and important in the West—of preaching. A great sexual sermon . . . has swept through our societies over the last decades" (7). Madonna, the Rolling Stones, and installments of "Seinfeld" devoted to the theme of masturbation are all possible, Foucault would say, because sex has finally become discourse.

Foucault is, as he and his postmodern peers have a habit of being, only half-right. (The lasting value of postmodern theory may be its ability to wring from us the long overdue Socratic admission that being half-right is all we can hope for.) In fact, one of those postmodern peers, Jean Baudrillard, points out that Foucault has missed the mark: "one must completely turn round what Foucault has to say in *The History of Sexuality I*, while still accepting its central hypothesis. Foucault sees only the *production* of sex as discourse" (1990a:47). Baudrillard wants to replace *production* with *seduction*, which he says "is stronger than production. It is stronger than sexuality, with which it must never be confused." Sex still becomes discourse, according to Baudrillard; that much Foucault got right. "The secret of all seduction," Baudrillard says as if he were commenting on "The Diary of the Seducer" or the *Symposium*, is the "transsubstantiation of sex into signs" (13). But because discourse is, on Baudrillard's view, simulation rather than power, sex does not become discourse by putting out, but by getting out. Instead of diving into the power structure of confession, sex surfaces in the hyperreal.

Baudrillard reiterates the repressive hypothesis, but with a twist: repression is not a function of power. Hyperreality "gives you so much—colour, lustre, sex, all in high fidelity, and with all the accents (that's life!)—that you have nothing to add, that is to say, nothing to give in exchange. Absolute repression: by giving you *a little too much* one takes away everything" (30). If for Foucault sex has become discourse because only in that way can we master it, for Baudrillard sex has become discourse because we have seen it a few too many times on cable. Free circulation undercuts production. Sex has been absorbed by discourse for the same reason music has been absorbed by high fidelity. We all have cd players now, but we don't play the cello anymore, and our enjoyment of music on cd is not enjoyment of music but of technical perfection. Similarly, we all seduce, but we do not have sex, and when we do seduce, we are not by any means fulfilling desire.

Baudrillard moves toward an integrative view with his idea of reversibility, but he is still, like Foucault, only half-right. We have made sex into discourse not, as Foucault contends, by the unidirectional act of transmutation, as alchemists tried to make lead into gold, nor, as Baudrillard contends, by the *potentially* bidirectional act of dissolution, as one dissolves a chlorine tablet into water, but by the *fully* bidirectional act of equivalence, as mathematicians can make 2 + 2 into 4, and 4 back into 2 + 2. Sex has not become discourse in the sense in which by its transformation it has been eliminated or dissolved; it has become discourse in the sense in which discourse has simultaneously become sex. When Derrida said there was *nothing* outside the text, he was not kidding.

The resolution to Bill Clinton's promised removal of the military ban on gays illustrates the point. That both groups of the disputants could accept a "don't ask, don't tell" policy, shows that what is at stake is not deviation in practice or in preference, but in prattle. Those in favor of removing the ban were happy that homosexual discourse was not excommunicated, and those in favor of retaining the ban were happy that homosexual discourse was kept sotto voce, but everyone knew from the beginning that neither homosexual acts nor homosexual desires could be excluded: the issue was whether homosexual discourse could be.

The paradigmatic sexual phenomena of our time are the dating service and the personal ad. It is too dangerous these days to exchange bodily fluids, and we have lost interest in exchanging things like "commitment" or what Wendell Berry calls "community," so we exchange text. We may fit ourselves to the text:

My Social Situation Is:

❑ I am new to this area
❑ I do not meet enough quality individuals
❑ I am too busy to look around
❑ I have not been on a date in _____ months

My Primary Social Goal Is:

❑ To date a lot
❑ To have a steady relationship
❑ To get married

Or we may fit the text to ourselves:

DWPM, 40s, 5'10", 160 lbs., financially secure, good-looking, non-smoker, drug-free, creative, funny, intelligent, caring Gemini, enjoys movies, music, dining out, or quiet evenings at home. Seeks slim, educated, passionate S/DWF, 20-30 for friendship, companionship, possibly romance, and perhaps long-term relationship. # 2032

Blond, attractive, submissive SWPM, late 20s, seeks imaginative, dominant SWF (age unimportant) whom I may worship, pay tribute to, and serve. Like bondage role playing games. Do whatever you want with me. # 1822

Either way, the medium of exchange is text.

Sex and discourse both occupy the position in our culture that fire held for Heraclitus's cosmology: "All things are requital for fire, and fire for all things, as goods for gold and gold for goods" (Kahn 47). Or, to borrow a modern analogue, sex and discourse resemble energy and matter in Einstein's physical theory: either can be transformed into the other. As energy and matter are equivalent, so are sex and discourse. A stricture, though, governs the exchange. On Foucault's view, the transformation of sex into discourse results in the addition of a surplus value, power, and on Baudrillard's view the transformation results in the subtraction of that same surplus value. Both are mistaken: the exchange is a strict equivalence, in which surplus value is neither generated nor lost.

The difference between Foucault's and Baudrillard's views of the transformation of sex into discourse and the view I am suggesting can be illustrated by comparison with the two forms of the circulation of commodities elucidated by Marx in *Capital*. In the simplest, C—M—C, a commodity (linen, to use one of Marx's examples) is exchanged for money, which is then exchanged for another commodity (a Bible). In this good form of circulation, money is merely money, the medium of an exchange without remainder. In the other form, M—C—M, money is exchanged for a commodity, which is then exchanged for more money. But the double entendre of "more" explains why Marx thinks this form of circulation is bad: one exchanges not only for *different* money than that with which one initially purchased the commodity, but for a *greater quantity* of money than that with which one purchased it. "The circuit M—C—M would be absurd and without meaning if the intention were to exchange by this means two equal sums of money, £100 for £100" (446). The two Cs in the first form of exchange are equal, but the two Ms in the second are unequal. "The exact form of this process is therefore M—C—M', where M' = M + ΔM = the original sum advanced, plus an increment" (448). Because this form of circulation creates surplus value, in it money is not only money but also capital, the catalyst of a cancerous exchange.

Foucault and Baudrillard both see the transformation of sex into discourse on analogy with M—C—M circulation. Foucault sees sex as a commodity exchanged in the circuit power—sex—discourse, in which the discourse is a form of power charged with surplus value. Baudrillard sees the process in reverse, as production—sex—seduction, or (equivalently) reality—sex—appearance, in which the surplus value of reality is dissipated, resulting in less than the origin instead of more. Actually, though, postmodern sex becomes discourse on analogy with C—M—C circulation, or as Lyotard expresses it, "there is no notable difference between a libidinal formation and a discursive formation" (1993:25).

No surplus value is created or lost when sex becomes discourse, because the medium of exchange, desire, like Marx's money, wants not to stay itself but to become something else, unlike Marx's capital, which wants to remain itself and increase. Christianity and capitalism did manage to transform sex into discourse, as Foucault contends, but only because their equivalence is already written into the insatiable polymorphousness of desire. Desire becomes discourse as readily as it becomes sex. We, like Pound's Bastidides and Baker's Jim and Abby, talk about sex all the time because all talk, as Freud showed us, is sexual. The postmoderns have only shown us the other side of the Freudian claim: all sex is discursive. If, as F. Gonzalez-Crussi puts it, using love as a euphemism for sex, "love is the supreme lexicographer" (162), for postmodernism the reverse also holds: lexicography is the supreme lover.

11 Postmodern Virtue

*Virtue is of so little regard in these costermongers' times
that true valor is turned bearherd. Pregnancy is made a
tapster, and hath his quick wit wasted in giving reckon-
ings. All the other gifts appertinent to man, as the malice
of this age shapes them, are not worth a gooseberry.*
—Shakespeare, 2 King Henry IV

No crisis of conscience has been portrayed more graphically than
that of the biblical character Job. Productive, prosperous, respected,
confident of his own virtue, and secure in the knowledge of his god's
favor, he was a nonpareil of moral security, in action how like an
angel, in apprehension how like a god. His happiness betokened his
virtue, as did his wealth; his virtue benefitted those he loved; and his
future seemed to promise only further abundance. Achilles for all his
renown had to capitulate to Agamemnon, and had to live with the
foreknowledge of his own demise; Socrates for all his integrity had
no home life and lived in poverty; Judith for all her valor brought
Holofernes' head back to a community that showed its gratitude by
condemning her to an otherwise empty life; no hero or heroine from
classical Western literature could claim a better life than the Job of
the Prologue. He was, or seemed to be, the beauty of the world, the
paragon of animals. But his claims to virtue were undercut by a
series of unanticipated tragedies. The herds that represented his
wealth were taken from him, as were the health that represented
his happiness and the children who represented his immortality.
His friends and his wife (the only surviving member of his family)
condemned him. All that surrounded him signified guilt in the moral
language of his time, yet his feelings and his own judgments insisted
he had done nothing wrong. He was a tragic figure without a tragic
flaw. He proved in the end no more than the quintessence of dust.

Blameworthy things had happened, but there was no one to whom he could attribute the blame. Job discovered that his moral language was insufficient to his circumstances: because he could not describe his situation, he could not understand it. "I have spoken of great things which I have not understood" (42:3). And because he could not understand his situation, he could not change it. Nothing remained for him but the silence of despair: "What reply can I give thee, I who carry no weight? / I put my finger to my lips" (40:4).

Contemporary culture is experiencing a similar crisis of conscience, as a glance at representative works of recent literature will confirm. Zeus transformed himself into a shower of gold to seduce Danaë and a swan to rape Leda; Gregor Samsa, in contrast, "awoke one morning from uneasy dreams" to find himself transformed, by unspecified causes and for no reason he could understand, "into a gigantic insect" (Kafka 1961:67). In 1854 Tennyson could ask about the "noble six hundred" who rode "Into the jaws of Death, / Into the mouth of hell" but were not dismayed, "When can their glory fade?" (226-27). Not seventy years later, Eliot could only say of the faceless workers walking over London Bridge "under the brown fog of a winter dawn" that "I had not thought death had undone so many" (1970:55). A century after the Light Brigade, Jack Gilbert wrote of the Poles who "rode out from Warsaw against the German tanks on horses" that although their act is beautiful and disquieting, "yet this poem," in contrast to Tennyson's paean in praise of the noble six hundred, "would lessen that day" (3). Boccaccio portrays a group of young men and women, in the middle of a plague that killed over half the citizens of Florence, telling stories of love and happiness; Camus, living in an age of unprecedented medical advance, creates an imaginary plague as a metaphor for his moral circumstances: the citizens of Camus's Oran are "hostile to the past, impatient of the present, and cheated of the future" (69). The twentieth century learned to say with the Nijinsky of Frank Bidart's poem: "The GUILT comes from NOWHERE" (6).

Job lost seven thousand sheep, a few hundred yoke of oxen, a "large number" of slaves, and his children. We have lost millions of soldiers in subhuman conditions in World War I, six million Jews to inhuman treatment in World War II, great leaders like Gandhi and Martin Luther King to assassinations, and if some of us still have our children, we have stolen their future, in the form of the oil reserves and the rain forests and the ozone layer of the world. We have constructed weapons with which we can annihilate civilization in one blow, and machines with which we are slowly asphyxiating the earth. The ancient Greeks left a legacy of thinkers like Plato and Aristotle, and lasting images like the Winged Victory and the Kritios Boy; the Middle Ages left a legacy of systematizers like Thomas Aquinas, and lasting images like Notre Dame and the Louvre; the Renaissance left a legacy of creators like Leonardo, discoverers like Galileo and Magellan, and images like the Mona Lisa and Michelangelo's David. The twentieth-century's legacy will be a legacy of survivors: refugees and hostages and prisoners of war, Anne Franks and Alexander Solzhenitsyns. Our lasting images will record not our glory but our disgrace: a lone student confronting a line of tanks in Tiananmen Square; a naked, napalmed Vietnamese orphan.

Everything conspires to make us feel guilty, in spite of our best intentions and our protestations of innocence. Like Job's, our moral language is insufficient to our situation. And like Job, our response has been to strive toward silence. The call to silence that ends the *Tractatus*, a book partially composed during Wittgenstein's service on the front in World War I, is no accident. If Augustine spoke for the Middle Ages when he said to his god that we are restless until we rest in you, Robert Bly spoke for the twentieth century when he wrote to no one in particular "I want to go down and rest in the black earth of silence."

The causes of our changed situation lie in problems unique to our century. One such twentieth-century problem is the technological exaggeration of human powers beyond anything the citizens of previous centuries would have thought possible. We can destroy ourselves collectively with nuclear warheads, or individually with carbon monoxide. We can replace a defective heart with a healthy one—or an artificial one. A woman can leave her father in Kansas City on one day, and be at her Peace Corps assignment in Cameroon on the next. She can call him when she arrives, and talk to him as if they were still holding hands. A taxpayer in his living room in North Dakota can watch Congress find new ways to waste his money. A Shakespeare scholar can ask her computer to find a particular passage for her by scanning the *Complete Plays* on a compact disk hardly bigger than her palm. As one's power increases, so does one's influence, and as one's influence increases, so does one's responsibility— yet our moral powers have not increased to accommodate our increased physical and social powers. The mass media are one source of power that might prima facie be regarded, in view of their capacity for providing information, as exclusively beneficial; yet as Czeslaw

Milosz writes, "citizens in a modern state, no longer mere dwellers in their village and district, know how to read and write but are unprepared to receive nourishment of a higher intellectual order. They are sustained artificially on a lower level by television, films, and illustrated magazines—media that are for the mind what too small slippers were for women's feet in old China" (109). We are slaves who have been given freedom and wealth, but have no one to teach us how to use it. Like Electra's peasant husband in Euripides' play or Ophelia in the first acts of *Hamlet*, we have been given something we cannot merit. We love it, but because it is greater than ourselves, it threatens to destroy us.

Another twentieth-century problem is that our world is now famously fast-paced and small. Job despaired because he had counted on a traditional, customary moral idea, held by his parents and their parents and their parents—namely, that God rewards the good and punishes only the bad—but his situation no longer fit into the picture his grandparents' ideas painted. For us, too, moral ideals have always been grounded in tradition and custom (the mores that give us the term *moral*), but in a world in which one can call Moscow on a phone made in Korea while driving a German car through Minneapolis, nothing is customary. In a world where teenagers arrive at college knowing who Madonna and Bart Simpson are, but not Portia and Alexander the Great, tradition has evaporated.

In a world without tradition and custom, without coherent, consistent moral communities, we are no longer given moral ideals, so those of us who yearn for them must discover or construct them. Left only with what Camus calls "lucidity," we must create a moral language that clarifies our situation. Then even if our choice of ideals is arbitrary, we will choose from among a set of clearly delineated alternatives, and even if we no longer speak, our silence will result from will, not despair.

The emotional situation of the late twentieth century can also be construed as an intellectual situation. In the *Critique of Practical Reason*, Kant described as necessary conditions for meaningful moral discourse and binding moral imperatives three postulates: immortality, freedom, and the existence of God. In 1788 Kant and his contemporaries could believe in all three, but for us and our contemporaries each is implausible. Belief in these postulates is made impossible not only by the declarations of the philosophers that God is dead and that religion is the opiate of the masses, but also by the declarations of the psychologists that the "faith in undetermined psychical events and in free will . . . is quite unscientific and must yield to the demand of a determinism whose rule extends over mental life" (Freud 1977:106), and that "if anyone makes a breach . . . in the determinism of natural events at even a single point, it means that he has thrown overboard the whole *Weltanschauung* of science" (28).

Belief in Kant's postulates is made impossible not only by the scientists' increasing subsumption of events under causality, as evidenced by chaos theory, but even by the defensive posture of popular religion, once the haven for such beliefs, which has followed theologians like Bultmann, Buber, and Tillich in abandoning the content of dogma to preserve its form. A glance at the titles on the religion shelf at the bookstore will reveal that even if the religious have not abandoned their beliefs, they at least know they should have: *God the Problem, The Christian Agnostic, But That I Can't Believe!* In the nineteenth century, science had to try to overcome religion; in the twentieth century, the burden of proof shifted.

Belief in any of Kant's three postulates now signifies a particular mental state: despair, a lack of education, or both. The French existentialists' insistence on human freedom of will responds to "absurdity" or despair. Televangelism targets the infirm and uneducated, in its more caricatured forms expecting people to respond to the preacher's instructions to be healed by touching the television screen as if, in Philip Larkin's words, an "idiot child within them still survives." Thus a belief structure like apocalypticism, which conjoins the three postulates, becomes ironic, as in Jim Harrison's "I think Jesus will return and the surprise will be / fatal" (90), or Kierkegaard's parable: "It happened that a fire broke out backstage in a theater. The clown came out to inform the public. They thought it was a jest and applauded. He repeated his warning, they shouted even louder. So I think the world will come to an end amid general applause from all the wits, who believe that it is a joke" (1971:30).

Contemporary moral beliefs typically either insist in spite of everything that freedom, immortality, and the existence of God are true postulates, and that therefore morality is safely grounded; or they accept that the postulation of freedom, immortality, and the existence of God is no longer plausible, and assume that morality must disappear with them into an abyss of nihilism. I will explore a third alternative: by acknowledging the implausibility of Kant's assumption that the postulates are necessary for morality, to clear a space for a careful investigation of the grounds for moral beliefs; and by drawing on the vocabulary of postmodernism, to work toward the creation of a moral language capable of describing and confronting the contemporary emotional and intellectual situation of humans.

In spite of accusations that it lacks rigor, postmodern theory in all its forms (structuralism, deconstruction, and the like), models itself, like other major movements in the humanities in this century, on science. My appropriation of some of the vocabulary of postmodern theory, then, attempts to make the language of ethics adequate to our "postmodern condition" by making ethics "scientific": not in the sense of the term used to group disciplines like physics and biology that share a methodology, but in the etymological sense that connotes rigorous, classificatory investigation of a subject, the sense in which Pound and Zukofsky describe the arts as science, and in which Northrop Frye wants to make literary criticism scientific, offering to the squeamish the synonyms "systematic" and "progressive" (7-8). This chapter thus will be an anatomy not only in the dictionary sense, "a dissection of something in order to determine the position, structure, etc. of its parts," but also in the sense given by Frye in the Glossary to his *Anatomy of Criticism*, namely "a form of prose *fiction* . . . characterized by a great variety of subject-matter and a strong interest in ideas" (365). I have italicized the word fiction to emphasize that in what follows I use Aristotle, Mill, Kant, Nietzsche, and others the way Plato used Socrates: not as the subjects of their own histories, but as characters in my story.

1. Virtue

In pre-twentieth-century Western ethical discourse, the usual procedure has been to seek a single rule or ideal (what I call an ethical canon), the proper application of which will answer any moral question or solve any moral problem, and by appeal to which alone any particular moral claim can be justified. Unfortunately, any such canon will be self-contradictory; unless tempered by the application of a competing canon, it will reduce itself to absurdity.

Propriety

By starting his investigation into ethics with an examination of commonly held views on the subject, Aristotle reveals that in his ethical theory he claims to be articulating a general principle or canon that people already know, whether or not they apply that knowledge, could formulate it, or are even conscious of it. He does so for the same reason Paul appealed in his Areopagus speech to the Unknown God, and for the same reason scientists revel in correlations between mathematical equations and observable phenomena: we assume that ethical laws, like divine laws and natural laws, must be discovered, not invented. Aristotle says he is not giving his readers a new ethical canon, only iterating a preexisting one.

The assumption that ethical views are discovered rather than invented Aristotle inherited from his preceptors. Socrates' maieutic method assumes the presence of all knowledge within the learner: instruction consists not in putting knowledge into the learner, but in drawing it out. The dialogic form of Plato's work is Socratic maieutics on paper. Nor should the Socratic / Platonic claim that knowledge is virtue mislead one: not knowledge itself is missing in those who are not virtuous because they do not "know" what is virtuous, but the instruction that actualizes knowledge. Even the ignorant have knowledge in their tank; they just need someone like Socrates to start their engines. As Socrates says after discussing geometry with Meno's slave, "not knowing" can be formulated more precisely as "not remembering at the moment" (Plato 86b).

Not that Aristotle thinks people make no ethical mistakes. He points out, for instance, that the many give wrong answers to the question of what happiness is: they "think it is something obvious and evident, e.g. pleasure, wealth or honour, some thinking one thing, others another; and indeed the same person keeps changing his mind, since in sickness he thinks it is health, in poverty wealth" (1095a). Yet, although they are wrong about the particular nature of happiness, they do correctly recognize the general principle that happiness is the highest good. Even individuals, like the incontinent and the immature, who do not appear to know the general principle, still know what they need to know; their flaw consists in following their desires and their feelings, respectively, instead of their reason.

The ethical canon Aristotle announces is propriety, which defines the good as the orderly, the appropriate. A good action matches the agent who performs it. In its most general terms, "the good, i.e. [doing] well, for a flautist, a sculptor, and every craftsman, and, in general, for whatever has a function and [characteristic] action, seems to depend on its function" (1097b). This general principle can be applied in any particular case. Therefore, "the virtue of eyes, e.g., makes the eyes and their functioning excellent, because it makes us see well; and similarly, the virtue of a horse makes the horse excellent, and thereby good at galloping, at carrying its rider and at standing steady in the face of the enemy." In the specific case of humans, then, "the virtue of a human being will likewise be the state that makes a human being . . . perform his function well" (1106a). The human function is, famously, the expression in activity of reason, since Aristotle believes (as only an ancient Athenian and not a contemporary American could believe), that humans are rational animals.

The canon of propriety guides even the apparently independent doctrine of the mean, often viewed, mistakenly, as the central tenet of Aristotle's ethics. Virtue seeks the mean "relative to us" (1106b), not an absolute or independent mean. In other words, the virtuous person seeks in the mean not an average of the available options, but the proportion appropriate to that person. Milo has the same range of alternatives at the Golden Corral that you and I have, but we should not order what he orders, because the quantity of food appropriate for Milo's consumption is not appropriate for ours. Similarly, Milo has the same range of alternatives at the Grolier that you and I have, but he should not try to read all that we read, because that would make him late for wrestling practice.

Aristotle is not proposing a relativistic theory, though. The mean is relative to the agent only in the sense of being different for different agents. It is *not* relative to the agent in the sense of being what the agent wants it to be or decides it is. For any one agent, in regard to any one virtue, there will be only one mean, about which the agent can err. Further, Aristotle gives a nonrelativistic standard for determining the mean—namely, the understanding of the intelligent person. In his definition of virtue, he stipulates that it is "defined by reference to reason, i.e., to the reason by reference to which the intelligent person would define it" (1107a). You and Milo should not eat the same amount, but the issue is how much nutrition you need, not merely what you are in the mood for. Jenny Craig has made a fortune from the fact that you can be wrong about how much you should eat. Not your desires or your feelings but your nature determines the mean relative to you.

The most obvious problem with a natural law ethical theory like Aristotle's is that crucial words like "nature" and "purpose" are ambiguous. The most serious problem, though, is that the theory buckles regardless of the definition chosen for those terms. Burton

Leiser's discussion of natural law arguments against homosexuality in *Liberty, Justice, and Morals* offers a particularly vivid demonstration of the way in which the canon of propriety, unless tempered by the application of an additional canon, reduces itself to absurdity. He identifies several possible meanings of the terms *natural* and *unnatural*, and then shows that as part of an argument against homosexuality each definition fails. *Natural* cannot mean "in conformity with the laws of nature," since the laws of nature are descriptive, not prescriptive. They describe "the manner in which physical substances *actually behave*" (51), rather than prescribing how they should behave. Thus, anything that does in fact happen, including homosexual activity, is natural in this sense of the term. Were this the definition of *natural*, and were being natural a sufficient condition for being good, everything would be good. *Unnatural* cannot mean that something is "a product of human artifice," since many products of human artifice are "better than what is natural" (52). For example, an artificially made down jacket from L. L. Bean keeps humans warm better than the natural mechanism of shivering. Therefore, even homosexuality's being unnatural in this sense would be no indication that it was wrong. *Unnatural* cannot mean something uncommon or abnormal, since many uncommon things, like Leiser's example of playing viola in a string quartet, are good. Finally, and most damaging to Aristotle, *unnatural* cannot mean contrary to the principal purpose or function of a thing. "A hammer," Leiser points out, "may have been designed to pound nails, and it may perform that particular job best. But it is not [wrong] to employ a hammer to crack nuts" (54). Similarly, the eyes, as Aristotle pointed out, are for seeing, but as Leiser points out, they may also be used for flirting.

Aristotle does give a criterion for determining the natural function of a thing—namely, what is unique to it. He infers that the purpose of humans is neither nutrition and growth, which they share with other living things, nor sense perception, which they share with animals, but reason, which only humans possess. However, Leiser observes that Aristotle's uniqueness criterion cannot adequately ground a moral canon. The human genitals are unique in their ability to generate new human beings, and not unique in their ability to give pleasure or express love. Yet "even the most ardent opponents of 'unfruitful' intercourse admit" that the genitals can appropriately give pleasure and express love, having "conceded that a man and his wife may have intercourse even though she is pregnant, or past the age of child bearing, or in the infertile period of her menstrual cycle" (55). The unique ability of the genitals to facilitate procreation does not determine which of their possible uses are appropriate.

The problem is that appropriateness can be determined, and Aristotle's canon applied, only by the simultaneous application of some other canon. For example, use of the genitals by a mutually consenting couple to express love is appropriate not because expressing love is natural or a unique capacity of the genitals, but because of the canon I will later call parity: it treats all relevant parties as possessing equal worth, and does only what benefits (or is perceived to benefit) all concerned. Use of the genitals by one person to have intercourse with a nonconsenting person is wrong, not because it is unnatural or a capacity not unique to the genitals, but because it violates the canon of parity. Aristotle whispering in one ear will help me become a better person only if John Stuart Mill whispers in the other.

Unchecked by the application of other canons, Aristotle's principle of propriety results in what I would call the *"Brave New World* syndrome." In Huxley's novel, citizens are grouped by purpose into castes called Alphas, Betas, Gammas, Deltas, and Epsilons, and they are modified during the process of "decanting" (birth having been rendered obsolete) according to what is appropriate for the members of the group to which they are destined. High intelligence is not appropriate to Epsilons, the physical labor caste, so their embryos are given less oxygen in order to remain below par. The explanation offered a dull student by the Director of Hatcheries perfectly applies the canon of appropriateness: "Hasn't it occurred to you that an Epsilon embryo must have an Epsilon environment as well as an Epsilon heredity?" (9). Epsilons, he says, "don't need human intelligence," and therefore should not possess it. The Director of Hatcheries only regrets that as yet nothing can remove the "long years of superfluous and wasted immaturity" between age ten, when the Epsilon mind is mature, and age eighteen, when the Epsilon body is mature and fit for work. Were propriety the only ethical canon, nothing would be wrong with the society depicted in *Brave New World*. That society is obviously bad only because we apply other canons to it.

Purity

Like Aristotle, Kant claims to be announcing a canon people already use, rather than constructing a new one. "All moral concepts," he says, "have their seat and origin completely a priori in reason, and indeed in the most ordinary human reason just as much as in the most highly speculative" (1981:22-23). Were this not true, morality could not be binding, since it would be grounded in "empirical, and hence merely contingent, cognition" (23). In such a case, morality would bind only those who had undergone the requisite experiences, not all humans.

Kant says that people use not Aristotle's canon of propriety, but an altogether different canon, purity. The good according to Kant is the internally consistent, the rational. He begins the *Grounding* with a criticism of Aristotle's canon. Moderation is "good in many respects," he says, but not "good without qualification," because without a good will moderation can "become extremely bad; for the coolness of a villain makes him not only much more dangerous but also immediately more abominable in our eyes than he would have been regarded by us without it" (7). Coolness in a villain meets Aristotle's canon of being appropriate to the person, but by application of another canon we recognize it as also morally bad. Kant's solution is to exclude the nature of the agent from consideration, and produce a canon that depends not on the *external purpose* the action serves, but on the *internal origin* of the action. Thus the worth of an action is kept from depending on "the effect expected from it" or on "any principle of action that needs to borrow its motive from this expected effect" (13).

Kant calls his canon the categorical imperative, and he first formulates it in this way: "I should never act except in such a way that I can also will that my maxim should become a universal law" (1981:14). His paradigm is promise-making. I know I should not make a promise I cannot keep, because I cannot universalize the maxim of the action, or in other words because the maxim contradicts itself. "I can indeed will the lie but can not at all will a universal law to lie. For by such a law there would really be no promises at all," since no one would believe me anymore, and no one would keep their promises to me. "Therefore, my maxim would necessarily destroy itself just as soon as it was made a universal law" (15).

Not the action's consequences but its nature makes the action wrong. Were consequences the problem, the wrongness of the action would be contingent on its actually having those consequences. My knowledge of the wrongness of the action would depend on my having particular experiences, and would therefore be empirical, not "pure." If I am truthful from "fear of disadvantageous consequences," I must "look around elsewhere to see what are the results for me that might be connected with the action," but if I am truthful from duty, "the concept of the action itself contains a law for me" (15). Further, not the nature of the agent, as in Aristotle, but the nature of the action, determines the action's worth. The action does not have to be appropriate to me, but to the law. For an action to be good, its maxim must be appropriate for everyone. If I should not make promises with the intention of breaking them, Milo should not either. In addition, I need not appeal to the imagined decision of *the* intelligent person for validation; if I am *an* intelligent (that is, rational) person, the validity of the decision will be evident to me.

Appealing to internal consistency as one's ethical canon certainly solves some of the problems associated with appealing to a correlation between the agent and the action, but not without raising other problems. For instance, purity as a canon cannot adjudicate between conflicting duties. One adjudicates between conflicting duties in precisely the same way one solves the problems of Aristotle's canon of propriety: by appealing to another canon. When, in the textbook example, I promise to hide a friend who appears at my door asking me to help him escape from his lover's enraged husband, I will have conflicting duties once the beweaponed husband appears and asks whether the friend is in my house. I have the duty not to lie, and the duty not to cooperate in a murder. Of course I know immediately which duty I will choose to fulfill, but my knowledge comes not from the canon of purity but from the canon I call parity, which tells me to choose the action that respects all concerned individuals and furthers the interests of all concerned.

Unchecked by the application of other canons, Kant's principle of purity results in the "'Modest Proposal' syndrome." In Jonathan Swift's satire, the narrator proposes a scheme "for preventing the children of poor people in Ireland from being a burden to their parents or country, and for making them beneficial to the public" (2144). The scheme is that poor infants "be offered in sale to the persons of quality and fortune through the kingdom," since the narrator has been told "by a very knowing American" that "a young healthy child well nursed is at a year old a most delicious, nourishing, and wholesome food, whether stewed, roasted, baked, or boiled" (2146). Nothing in the maxim of this action would "destroy itself" if universalized; it is not internally inconsistent. We will not run out of babies, for instance, since more can always be made, so eating babies is not inconsistent for the reason using fossil fuels or destroying the habitat of the spotted owl is inconsistent. Nor is it hyperbole to say that no inconsistency undercuts Swift's proposal, since Kant implies as much himself. Swift tells us, as justification for a three-to-one ratio between females and males in those "reserved for breed," that "these children are seldom the fruits of marriage" anyway. Subtracting the irony from Swift leaves Kant:

> A child that comes into the world apart from marriage is born outside the law (for the law is marriage) and therefore outside the protection of the law. It has, as it were, stolen into the commonwealth (like contraband merchandise), so that the commonwealth can ignore its existence (since it rightly should not have come to exist in this way), and can therefore also ignore its annihilation. (1991:144-45)

We know, of course, that something is wrong with the policies of eating poor infants and disregarding the death of a child born into a toilet bowl in a public high school in Nashville. But we know on the basis of another canon, not the canon of purity. We know by appeal, again, to parity, because the policies further the interests of some members of society, to the complete exclusion of the interests of others.

Parity

The principle of parity itself receives a vivid formulation in the writings of John Stuart Mill, notably in *Utilitarianism*. The good, according to Mill, is what includes everyone on an equal basis, what is fair. Like Aristotle and Kant, Mill claims to be announcing a canon already in use. The "steadiness" and "consistency" human moral beliefs have shown across time, Mill says, "has been mainly due to the tacit influence of a standard not yet recognized" (3). He ventures that his canon "has had a large share in forming the moral doctrines even of those who most scornfully reject its authority." Even opponents of utilitarianism, he maintains, are unwitting utilitarians.

As Kant criticized Aristotle by saying that Aristotle's canon of propriety ultimately led to Kant's own canon of purity, so Mill criticizes Kant by saying that Kant's canon leads to Mill's. When Kant applies the categorical imperative, Mill says, "he fails, almost grotesquely, to show that there would be any contradiction, any logical (not to say physical) impossibility, in the adoption by rational beings of the most outrageously immoral rules of conduct. All he shows is that the *consequences* of their universal adoption would be such as no one would choose to incur" (4). Mill's own canon he calls "the principle of utility" or "the greatest happiness principle," and formulates in this way: "actions are right in proportion as they tend to promote happiness; wrong as they tend to produce the reverse of happiness. By happiness is intended pleasure and the absence of pain; by unhappiness, pain and the privation of pleasure" (7).

Describing actions as right "in proportion" to something else is one clue that Mill's canon is more adept at choosing between conflicting obligations than at identifying categorical ones, since it makes right and wrong a matter of degree rather than an absolute. But Mill manages less than a page after formulating his principle until, like Aristotle and Kant before him, he has to call on another principle. Having stated that "pleasure and freedom from pain are the only things desirable as ends," he anticipates charges of Epicureanism. To treat pleasure as the highest good is, he anticipates his opponents saying, "utterly mean and groveling," a doctrine "worthy only of swine" (7). Mill's answer to these charges has always bothered his readers, because after having given a quantitative tool for assessing moral worth (amount of pleasure) he immediately adds a qualitative tool (type of pleasure), without appearing to give a criterion by which to distinguish between qualities of pleasures. But he does appeal to a criterion, tacitly at least, and it is precisely Aristotle's canon of propriety! "A beast's pleasures do not satisfy a human being's conceptions of happiness. Human beings have faculties more elevated than the animal appetites and, when once made conscious of them, do not regard anything as happiness which does not include their gratification" (8). Some pleasures, in other words, are appropriate to beasts, and some to humans; humans should seek the pleasures appropriate to their natures. Déjà vu. Mill even uses the same procedure Aristotle does to apply the canon— namely, to accept as authoritative the judgment of the most competent (real or imagined) person, with only the difference that Aristotle defines competence as intelligence, and Mill defines it as experience.

Mill's canon of parity can stand on its own no more than can Aristotle's canon of propriety or Kant's canon of purity. To say with Mill that when choosing between one's "own happiness and that of others," one must be "as strictly impartial as a disinterested and benevolent spectator" (16), raises the question of who or what will be included in the category of "others" and who or what will not. The canon of parity inevitably raises, but by itself cannot answer, that question.

Untempered by any other canon, parity results in the "Jainism syndrome." Jainism is "a sectarian offshoot of Hinduism" (Hardon 147), best known to Westerners for the importance it places on "the idea of 'non-hurting' of life (*Ahimsa*) irrespective of its distinction into higher and lower. . . . 'Hurt no one' is a sacred mandate which enjoins love and compassion for all living beings" (151). The Jaina ascetic follows the principle of parity all the way down the slippery slope, refusing for instance to run or jump, "so that he will avoid stepping on any creature no matter how small" (Jaini 247). In fact, all three major sects of Jainism "furnish their monks with something [a brush or a peacock's feather] with which they may sweep insects from their path" (Stevenson 227). Even lay people may take a vow that "forbids the killing of weak creatures like mosquitoes and any other troublesome insects" (206). And this concern for smaller organisms extends beyond the activity of walking: Jaina samiti, or rules of conduct, even enjoin "care in performing the excretory functions (*utsargasamiti*)—the place chosen must be entirely free of living things" (Jaini 248).

By following the canon of parity with more consistency than Mill mustered, Jainism reveals that parity cannot distinguish between entities that deserve moral consideration and those that do not, or even distinguish between entities that deserve more consideration and those that deserve less. That the pollution from driving my car to work would diminish my future quality of life and that of my nieces and nephews recommends biking to work instead; that a few grasshoppers would end up on the car's grill does not.

The more recent Western "animal rights" movement well illustrates the inability of the principle of parity to stand on its own. In *Animal Liberation*, Peter Singer argues, by appeal, he says, "to basic moral principles that we all accept" (iii), that the interests of animals deserve equal consideration with those of humans. Singer's concept of "speciesism" is an accusation of inconsistency: it claims that we have not followed through on our application of the principle of parity, which he assumes we all accept as our ethical canon. According to Singer, the decision to give equal consideration to the interests only of members of our own species is merely a prejudice. He correctly observes that the principle of parity demands "that our concern for others and our readiness to consider their interests ought not to depend on what they are like or on what abilities they may possess" (5), yet within two pages he has selected the others about which he will maintain concern precisely by an ability they possess—namely, the ability to experience pleasure and pain. Singer argues that "the limit of sentience . . . is the only defensible boundary of concern for the interests of others. To mark this boundary by some other characteristic like intelligence or rationality would be to mark it in an arbitrary manner" (8-9). But of course sentience is every bit as arbitrary a criterion as intelligence or rationality, as Singer himself reveals. At several points in the book, Singer addresses the question why we should include pigs and minks in our sphere of ethical concern but not cabbages or quartz crystals or even creatures like cockroaches that do not merit mention in his book. He answers that only animals like mammals and birds have interests to be considered; in other words, they are the only ones we *can* consider. But the same arbitrary claim has been used to justify other prejudices: racists have contended that Africans and their descendants cannot have interests, chauvinists have contended that women cannot have interests, and as Singer himself is fond of reminding us, Aristotle said slaves cannot have interests.

Singer's prejudice appeals to the same criterion as do the prejudices he (rightly) derides: beings count as having interests if and only if they are like us. How, according to Singer, do we know if something is suffering? If it acts like we do ("writhing, facial contortions, moaning," [1990:11]), and if it has a nervous system like our own. Singer has made a moral advance, but not the moral advance he claims for himself. He has expanded the domain of the "us" beyond only Caucasians or only males or only property-owners to the significantly larger domain of only vertebrates, but he has not supplied a nonarbitrary boundary for that domain. He has appealed for that boundary, like all those whose prejudices he criticizes, to a canon outside the one he recognizes—namely, the canon I call primacy.

Primacy

Nietzsche is the best example of an ethicist whose canon is primacy. For him, the good is what excels, what is superior to other things. He explicitly rejects parity, as for instance in this passage from *Twilight of the Idols*: "The doctrine of equality! There is no more poisonous poison anywhere: for it seems to be preached by justice itself, whereas it really is the termination of justice. 'Equal to the equal, unequal to the unequal'—*that* would be the true slogan of justice; and also its corollary: 'Never make equal what is unequal' (1968a:553). Nature grounds this rejection of parity, Nietzsche says. "Life itself recognizes no solidarity, no 'equal rights,' between the healthy and degenerate parts of an organism: one must excise the latter—or the whole will perish" (1968b:389). For Nietzsche, rights and privileges are not and should not be evenly distributed, but instead belong exclusively to the exceptional person, the strong one, the genius.

The justification of the canon of primacy is, in Nietzsche's formulation, that it liberates and thus leads to salubrity, unlike the other canons, which constrain and thus lead to atrophy. Nietzsche favors conflict, for instance, over peace, not because he follows Empedocles' acquiescence to conflict as an inescapable metaphysical presence, but on the more pragmatic ground that conflict reveals primacy and peace conceals it. He would have agreed with the father in Stephen Crane's poem:

> Are not they who possess the flowers
> Stronger, bolder, shrewder
> Than they who have none?
> Why should the strong—
> The beautiful strong—
> Why should they not have the flowers?

Although he criticized Darwin for preferring species to individuals, Nietzsche's use of primacy as a moral canon resembles the Darwinian notion that we know advantageous variations enable a creature to survive longer, because that is what advantageous means (Darwin 63-64).

Nietzsche's use of primacy as his moral canon explains not only his preference for conflict over peace, but also other ideas like his rejection of reason. He discards reason not on epistemological grounds, but on moral grounds. The problem is not that reason fails to uncover truth, but that it covers virtue. By placing the burden of proof on the knower, reason obligates the strong toward the weak. It subverts primacy. "What must first be proved is worth little. Wherever authority still forms part of good bearing, where one does not give reasons but commands, the dialectician is a kind of buf-

foon: one laughs at him, one does not take him seriously"
(1968a:476).

Unchecked by the application of any other canon, primacy
would entail the "Hitler syndrome," a view according to which,
because primacy dictates no responsibility toward others, no action is
in itself immoral. "An action in itself," Nietzsche says, "is perfectly
devoid of value: it all depends on *who* performs it" (1968b:165).
Primacy alone does not reveal anything wrong with Hitler's having
had millions of people slaughtered. The fact that he was powerful
enough to do so justifies the act. It is not surprising that Nietzsche
wanted humans to become like gods, since the principle of primacy
only extends to humans one answer to Socrates' question about the
gods in the *Euthyphro*. If something is holy because the gods love it,
the gods can never do wrong, because their tastes define right and
wrong. "If I am not *more* than the law, I am the vilest of all men,"
Nietzsche says (1982:15). In the *Genealogy of Morals*, Nietzsche formulates this in a parable when he says that lambs (applying the canon
of parity) will accuse raptors of evil for their habit of "bearing off little lambs," but because the birds of prey have no responsibility
toward the lambs, they will view the lambs' reaction "a little ironically and say: 'we don't dislike them at all, these good little lambs; we
even love them: nothing is more tasty than a tender lamb'" (480-81).

Nietzsche himself avoids the Hitler syndrome by a strategy
that should by now be predictable: he balances the canon of primacy
with another canon—namely, the canon of propriety we first saw
in Aristotle. The same parable of the lambs and raptors that illustrates primacy's failure to proscribe any actions, also shows that
Nietzsche *does* proscribe some actions. He does so by appeal to propriety. The bird of prey kills lambs because doing so is appropriate to
a bird of prey. Similarly, strong people do what is appropriate to
strong people. So Nietzsche infers from the parable that "to demand
of strength that it should not express itself as strength, that it should
not be a desire to overcome, a desire to throw down, a desire to
become master, a thirst for enemies and resistances and triumphs, is
just as absurd as to demand of weakness that it should express itself
as strength" (481). Kaufmann has argued at length that Nietzsche
opposes anti-Semitism, and that his ideas do not sanction the holocaust. My points are first that Nietzsche cannot object to the action
per se, only the agent, and second that the objection cannot be
grounded in an appeal to his explicitly avowed canon of primacy,
but only in an appeal to the tacitly present canon of propriety.

Why the Canons Failed

The problem with all these traditional views is, as I have tried to show, that a strict application of any one principle, untempered by the concurrent application of at least one of the others, invariably results in absurdity. In other words, as soon as ethical discourse seeks to become totalizing, it becomes tyrannical. There is no rule to which alone we can appeal for ethical justification without becoming victims of the rule. Is there then no beneficial ethical discourse available to us? Are we reduced to the silence into which modernism sinks? I think not, and wish to suggest that meaningful ethical discourse is possible, provided that even those of us who are "postmoderns" only reluctantly are willing to import discourse from our contemporaries in fields outside ethics.

Wittgenstein illustrates well the sense in which I mean that modernism saw ethics end in silence, and that postmodernism reopens ethical discourse. For the early Wittgenstein, semiology and axiology are mutually exclusive. Modern moral philosophy had been severely bludgeoned by Nietzsche already, but Wittgenstein neatly severs its jugular. If, as I argued in an earlier chapter, this intrepid pair tossed out the bath water that is freedom, they also tossed out the baby. The same extraordinary *Tractatus* passage, beginning at 6.4, that denies voluntary agency, also denies the possibility of meaningful moral discourse. If "all propositions are of equal value," then "the sense of the world must lie outside the world," and "it is impossible for there to be propositions of ethics." What philosophy with a hammer mortally wounded, philosophy with a sharp knife finished off: here lieth modern moral philosophy, *requiescat in pace*. So long as "the world divides into facts" (1961:1.2), a fact is "the existence of states of affairs" (2), and "a state of affairs (a state of things) is a combination of objects (things)" (2.01), there will be no space for value, and no meaningful ethical discourse. So long as language is strictly representational, so long as the only task it can perform is to convey facts, so long as its *telos* is Cartesian mathematical certainty and the Kantian synthetic a priori, value will be excluded from its domain, and there can be no meaningful ethical discourse.

Wittgenstein demonstrates how modern philosophy, like the biblical Job, let itself be silenced by the facts. When Jehovah reprimands Job out of the whirlwind, he might as well be quoting Wittgenstein. He says, in effect, that "in the world everything is as it is, and everything happens as it does happen." God made humans suffer, and there is nothing for Job to say. But had Job persisted in the alternative language use he engaged in prior to the whirlwind, imagining what was not the case (that he could bring God to court) instead of what was the case (that God, like the Athenians of Socrates' day, does not take kindly to being questioned), he would have seen that he should not have been silenced by the whirlwind. He would have seen that even though God *did not* make the world in such a way that humans do not suffer, God *could have*. Valuation depends not only on what is the case but also on what is not the case.

For the Wittgenstein of the *Investigations*, axiology instead of being excluded from semiology is subsumed by it. Language ceases to be univocal. In the *Investigations*, Wittgenstein acknowledges that "*Thought* can be of what is *not* the case" (1958a:94). Everything, including what is not the case, is language. He recognizes that events are not isolated and singular, but take place within, and share parameters with, systems. "To obey a rule, to make a report, to give an order, to play a game of chess, are *customs* (uses, institutions)." The English word *moral* comes, of course, from the Latin *mos* (pl. *mores*), meaning custom. These customs / uses / institutions are languages, to understand which "means to be master of a technique" (199). The structurality of language, combined with the flexibility and multivalence of its units, means that we must know how to adapt the use of our tools (words) to the demands of the task. For the late Wittgenstein, then, morality assumes the character of a language. This identity between the valuable and the significant is a prolegomenon to any future ethics.

Because he clings by his *Tractatus* toes to the very modernism he helped kill and at the same time clutches with his *Investigations* fingers the postmodernism he helped inaugurate, Wittgenstein forms a bridge. Following his favorite analogy of chess, my own thesis can be formulated in this way. Traditional ethicists have been asking for the principles of ethics to be like the rules for *playing* chess, what Stanley Cavell calls "defining rules" and "regulatory rules," but in fact ethical principles are more like the "rules" for *winning* at chess, or what Cavell calls "principles" and "maxims" (1979:305). The rules for playing chess are agreed on by all concerned parties, have been explicitly formulated, and are inviolable. I simply cannot move my rook diagonally. The rules for winning at chess are far more complex, however. The rules for playing chess can be completely formulated in a single reasonably slender book; in contrast, more books have been written about how to win at chess than on any other subject, without exhausting the topic. The topic is not, in fact, exhaustible: no list of rules for winning at chess will be either complete or inviolable. Every chess player knows not to trade a queen for a rook, yet every chess player dreams of the chance to make a winning queen sacrifice. Every chess player knows that in the opening the pieces should be developed before beginning an attack; yet every chess player has won games by violating that rule.

Mastery of chess does not consist in knowledge of a coherent set of rules. In fact, the rules for winning at chess (principles and maxims) are incoherent. The player who wins by violating the rule against attacking before developing her pieces was also following the rule that one should attack weaknesses in the opponent's position. The player had to choose between incompatible rules. A club player will beat a novice because the novice knows only the rules for playing, but few or none of the rules for winning. An expert will beat a club player because, while both know many of the rules for winning, the expert is more adept at applying them. A grandmaster will beat an expert because the grandmaster knows not only how to apply the rules for winning, but how and when to break them.

Cavell argues that only principles and maxims, but not regulatory or defining rules, operate in ethics. "No rule or principle," he says, "could function in a moral context the way regulatory or defining rules function in games. It is as essential to the form of life called morality that rules so conceived be absent as it is essential to the form of life we call playing a game that they be present" (307). To Cavell's conclusion I want to add that traditional Western moral theorists have been playing like amateurs: they have treated principles and maxims as if they were regulatory or defining rules. They have followed one principle (a bishop is worth the same as a knight) without tempering it by the application of others (bishops are more valuable in open positions, knights in closed ones; bishops are more valuable than knights in endgames with pawns on both sides of the board). An adequate moral theory, though, like mastery of chess, will have to acknowledge that the relevant principles are interdependent, each conditioned by others.

I do not assert that the canons I have discussed constitute an exhaustive list of the possibilities, nor that this manner of slicing the ethical pie is more proper or true than some other. Just the opposite. Plato, Spinoza, Schopenhauer, and G. E. Moore would have served the purpose. The point is this. Each of the ethical canons I have discussed fails to deliver sound moral judgments by itself, but not because of its proponent's inadequate articulation of it, nor because of some flaw shared only by these particular canons but not by some as yet unidentified canon. The canons *did* fail, but they failed because they *had to*. There is no possibility of our discovering (or creating or imposing) a single moral principle that will by itself provide sound moral direction. The approach shared by Western ethicists for more than twenty centuries was doomed to failure from the beginning, for reasons postmodern theorists make clear.

Lyotard gives one such reason in *The Differend*, where he distinguishes between what he calls a "litigation" and what he calls a "differend." A litigation is a conflict in which the parties agree on the rule or the mechanism of arbitration between their views. As the name suggests, a court case is a perfect example of a litigation: when I disagree with the owner of the rental house next door over the adequacy of his maintenance of the house, we agree that the opinion of the judge in civil court will settle our dispute. In contrast, a differend is "a case of conflict, between (at least) two parties, that cannot be equitably resolved for lack of a rule of judgment applicable to both arguments" (1988:xi). Thus when I disagree with my brother over whether humans were created by God in a special act of creation, we disagree not only on the answer, but also on the method of resolving that disagreement. In other words, in a litigation the conflict occurs within what Lyotard calls a "genre of discourse," and in a differend the conflict occurs between different genres of discourse. Each kind of conflict has its own kind of negative result. An unresolved litigation results in "damages." "Damages result from an injury which is inflicted upon the rules of a genre of discourse but which is reparable according to those rules" (xi). A "wrong" results from a differend, "from the fact that the rules of the genre of discourse by which one judges are not those of the judged genre or genres of discourse" (xi). Resolution to a differend is effected by power, and thus by what Lyotard elsewhere calls "terror": resolution occurs because one player in the language game threatens to eliminate the other, not because that player makes "a better 'move'" (1984:46).

Lyotard argues "that a universal rule of judgment between heterogeneous genres is lacking in general" (1988:xi). In a differend, whether the conflicting parties are person vs. person, person vs. society, or person vs. oneself, resolution can occur only by terror or by finding a rule that governs the rule each side is following. In other words, resolution can occur only by terror or by turning the differend into a litigation. A satisfactory resolution occurs, then, when the two conflicting rules are subsumed under a single, higher rule that governs them. When this higher, governing rule is called into question by conflict with another rule, the conflict can be resolved only by the subsumption of these two rules under a yet higher governing rule. And so on. Like the child's endless iteration of the question "Why?," which ends inevitably in "Because I'm your father, dammit," the subsumption of rules under other rules can end only *ad bauculum*, by what Lyotard calls terror.

A litigation is only a differend waiting to happen. There could be a final governing rule only if there were a rule that could not come into conflict with another rule, but there can be no such rule. As long as a rule can be questioned, as long, to return to Lyotard, "as the rule is what is at stake in the discourse, then the rule is not the rule of that discourse" (97). No rule can govern a genre of discourse without being part of that discourse, and no rule can be transcendent without being outside all genres of discourse. Therefore, there can be no transcendent governing principle. Lyotard says:

> The idea that a supreme genre encompassing everything that's at stake could supply a supreme answer to the key-questions of the various genres founders upon Russell's aporia. Either this genre is part of the set of genres, and what is at stake in it is but one among others, and therefore its answer is not supreme. Or else, it is not part of the set of genres, and it does not therefore encompass all that is at stake, since it excepts what is at stake in itself. . . . The principle of an absolute victory of one genre over another has no sense. (138)

What in an earlier chapter I called "postmodern aporesis" means that no single canon can, even in principle, govern ethics.

If we now recall that postmodern theorists (following the lead of moderns like Marx, Nietzsche, and Freud, who saw human actions as signs) treat value systems semiologically, as texts, it is easy to infer the need to treat ethical principles in the way the postmoderns teach us to treat texts, as a network rather than as a hierarchy. Roland Barthes contends that a text is "only a tissue of signs" (1977:147). Metaphors of depth, which imply hierarchy, must give way, he says, to metaphors of interconnection and interdependence. The structure of a text "can be followed, 'run' (like the thread of a stocking) at every point and at every level, but there is nothing beneath." As we must, according to Barthes, give up the dream of "a single 'theological' meaning" to texts, and recognize them as "a multi-dimensional space" inhabited by "a variety of writings" that "blend and clash" (146), so we must, I argue, give up the dream of a single, theological ethical principle, and recognize ethics as a multi-dimensional space inhabited by a variety of principles that blend and clash.

Derrida offers other reasons why the search for a supervening ethical principle must fail. *Of Grammatology* will serve as an example of the various arguments from his works by which he denies the possibility of totality. Although Derrida attends more directly and consistently to language as writing and speech than do Lyotard and Barthes, for both of whom political structure as language and language as legitimation tool are more interesting, he does make plain at the beginning of the *Grammatology* that his ideas extend at least to ethical structure as language: "the *problem of language* has never been simply one problem among others. But never as much as at present has it invaded, *as such*, the global horizon of the most diverse researches and the most heterogeneous discourses" (6).

Derrida deconstructs the privileging of speech over writing in such authors as Rousseau, Saussure, and Lévi-Strauss, supplanting (or supplementing) it with its opposite, a privileging of writing over speech. In doing so, he shows that speech was never, as its advocates longed for it to be, the locus of presence, and that writing was never merely "a particular, derivative, auxiliary form of language," never merely "the insubstantial double of a major signifier, *the signifier of the signifier*," but that on the contrary writing, rather than speech, "*comprehends* language" (7). That no signifier is not also a signified, and no signified not also a signifier, means, to translate into the vocabulary of ethics, that no rule is not also ruled. "There is not a single signified that escapes, even if recaptured, the play of signifying references that constitutes language," nor an ethical principle governing action that escapes being governed. The signifier, Derrida says, "cannot be a totality, unless a totality constituted by the signified preexists it, supervises its inscriptions and its signs, and is independent of it in its ideality" (18). Phonocentrism dreams of a signifier that presents the signified; Derridean grammatology recognizes that the signifier could present the signified only if it was already present. The signifier, in other words, could accomplish its function only under conditions that precluded the possibility of its functioning.

The same argument can be extended to the dream of a transcendent ethical principle: a transcendent ethical principle can be transcendent only if it is not ethical, and vice versa. Nor is such an argument unique to Derrida or postmodernism, reconstituting as it does the *Euthyphro* aporia: "Is what is holy holy because the gods approve it, or do they approve it because it is holy?" (10a). If the former, the holy is constituted by what precedes the holy (namely, the approval of the gods), because what constitutes the holy must precede the holy and therefore cannot itself be holy. If the latter, the holy must precede the approval of the gods, and therefore cannot be constituted by it. The approval of the gods, Euthyphro's transcendent principle for generating the holy, either generates the holy but is not itself holy, or is holy but does not generate the holy. It is transcendent but not principled, or else it is principled but not transcendent.

An analogous aporia manifests itself in forms of government. Either the will of the legislator (as in monarchy) precedes and is outside the law, and is able thus to constitute it, or the law (as in democracy) precedes and constitutes the will of the legislator, who is thus within the law. In other words, the law can either be made by the power of the legislator (something antecedent to and outside itself), or it can make (and include within itself) the power of the legislator. Law can be created only by the unlawful.

Applied to ethics, the sense of the Derridean claim that there is nothing outside the text can only be that, as "the alleged derivativeness of writing . . . was possible only on one condition: that the 'original,' 'natural,' etc. language had never existed, never been intact and untouched by writing, that it had itself always been a writing" (56), so ethics can be generated by a transcendent principle only on condition that the principle has never existed except as ethics itself. The answer to the question what makes the good good is not something outside goodness. To no transparent principle, no divine will analogous to our own, can opaque ethics be reduced. In the context of ethics, Derrida's claim that there is nothing outside the text amounts to a gloss on Wittgenstein's fragment, "just where one says 'But don't you see . . . ?' the rule is no use, it is what is explained, not what does the explaining" (1967:56). As John Tagg puts it, "Only discourses of dominance present themselves as unmarked, disembodied, self-identical and transcendent. . . . If justice sets bounds to the jurisdictions of language, it is not the domain of a court of appeal 'beyond' the pale of conflicting phrase regimens" (21, 25). What governs virtue might be power, but could not be virtue; anything that presented itself as a transcendent ethical principle could not be one.

Ethics without Canons

I have argued so far for three claims. First, that the ethical situation of postmodernity is unique, we and our ethical context having been irreversibly altered by technology, by cultural changes, by history, and so on. Second, that traditional ethical theory has been unable to accomplish its *telos*, the discovery or invention of a single prevenient ethical canon, each candidate having been found to depend for its own success on the concurrent application of another canon. Third, that postmodern theorists show why ethics not only has failed, but had to fail, its *telos* having proven self-contradictory.

A similar set of views leads John D. Caputo to argue against ethics. He rightly observes that "the principles we write are like the checks we write; their whole value depends upon what they have in their account. We do not really apply principles to individual 'cases,'" he says, but instead "we apply individuals to principles" (37). Are we, like the "faces along the bar" in Auden's poem, "lost in a haunted wood," never having "been happy or good"? Are we, like the travelers of Descartes' *Discourse*, lost in an ethical forest, with nothing to do but "walk as straight as they can in one direction," even though that direction was randomly chosen, only because "they will at least arrive somewhere at the end, where probably they will be better off than in the middle of the forest" (96)? I think not, but the *Discourse* passage serves as a reminder that where one cannot follow prior direction, one must deploy a strategy.

If there can be no governing rule, if no single canon is satisfactory, then we lack prior direction. Even knowing that we are to use some combination of the available canons does not solve the problem, since it does not supply us with a rule for how to combine them. It is like saying, "to beat Kasparov, only move your bishops diagonally and your rooks in straight line." True, but not much help. In the ethical realm one can only follow what computer scientists call "fuzzy logic." Engineers employ fuzzy logic to make machines that must operate according to criteria that are hard to define, like air conditioners that must cool air that feels "too hot" and warm air that feels "too cold":

When mathematicians lack specific algorithms that dictate how a system should respond to inputs, fuzzy logic can control or describe the system by using "commonsense" rules that refer to indefinite quantities. No known mathematical model can back up a truck-and-trailer rig from a parking lot to a loading dock when the vehicle starts from a random spot. Both humans and fuzzy systems can perform this nonlinear guidance task by using practical but imprecise rules such as "If the trailer turns a little to the left, then turn it a little to the right." (Kosko 76)

Systems that employ fuzzy logic can learn, and in many situations they can be *more* useful and accurate than standard mathematical systems.

The rules of ethics are as "practical but imprecise" as those used in backing up tractor trailer rigs, so a useful ethical strategy will be "fuzzy." Other ethicists, notably Aristotle, have tipped their hats toward fuzziness in ethics before ignoring it in pursuit of a principle. Other postmodern theorists have articulated the need for what I am calling fuzziness. Andrew Cutrofello, for example, reads Foucault as demanding in response to Kant a "juridical model of critique that would not itself be juridically modeled" (8). He recommends replacing a principle with a strategy.

If the categorical imperative is reinterpreted as a general strategy for subverting disciplinary matrices, it can serve as the basis for a very different sort of ethic from the one which Kant actually develops. Instead of issuing a set of decrees through the court of reason, the categorical imperative becomes, instead, a strategy for undermining those mechanisms that exercise a discipline of domination over bodies. (100)

If strategies are an-archic, they are not amorphous. Fortunately, among the concepts of postmodern theory are some that can move us toward the formulation of cogent "fuzzy" ethical strategies. Two such concepts are what Chomsky and Jonathan Culler call *competence* and what Lévi-Strauss calls *bricolage*.

Chomsky uses *competence* to address a fact about language that makes language similar to the postmodern ethical situation as I have described it. He calls the linguistic fact *creativity*, by which he means "the capacity that all native speakers of a language," even children of five and six, "have to produce and understand an indefinitely large number of sentences that they have never heard before and that may indeed never have been uttered before by anyone," and to do so despite being "generally unaware of applying any grammatical rules or systematic principles of formation" (Lyons 21). Similarly, human agents have a capacity to act ethically in an indefinitely large number of situations they have never encountered before, even without consciously applying rules. Humans are born, Chomsky says in a manner refreshingly reminiscent of the Socrates of the *Phaedo* and *Meno*, with an innate capacity to acquire competence in the language(s) with which they are surrounded during the first years of language learning. This competence enables humans to accommodate themselves to, and take advantage of, the creativity of language.

Chomsky defines competence in various ways, from "the cognitive state that encompasses all those aspects of form and meaning and their relation, including underlying structures that enter into that relation," to "a system of rules that generate and relate certain mental representations including in particular representations of form and meaning, the exact character of which is to be discovered" (90). But whether it is a cognitive state or a system of rules, the important point for a discussion of ethics is that grammatical competence enables "the speaker, in principle, to understand an arbitrary sentence and to produce a sentence expressing his thought" (201).

Others have made the comparison between grammar and ethical principles. John Rawls, for instance, cites Chomsky as part of his justification for his "idea of the original position." It resembles grammatical principles in that its being a theoretical construction that goes "much beyond the norms and standards cited in everyday life" (47) is no argument against it. Arthur Danto uses the same comparison in the process of making a point about artistic style. "Moral competence," he says, "is almost like linguistic competence, in the sense that the mark of the latter is the ability to produce and to understand novel sentences in the language. And no more than having linguistic competence can consist in having mastered a list of the sentences in a language can morality consist in having mastered a list of the right things to do" (202).

My own purpose is to emphasize that ethical principles resemble the rules of grammar in at least the sense that they are multiple rather than single. Neither English grammar nor ethics can be reduced to a single principle. Still, in spite of the occasional failures that distinguish performance from competence, native English speakers, even when they cannot formulate the rules they are using, are competent to distinguish grammatical from ungrammatical usage. Similarly, regardless of the failures in performance that Aristotle called incontinence, humans are competent to distinguish "grammatical" actions from "ungrammatical" ones.

Jonathan Culler argues for a similar competence in reading literature. He defines literary competence "as a set of conventions for reading literary texts" (118), although he clarifies that competence extends to the writing of literary texts as well as the reading of them. (Both writers and readers possess it, in other words.) Culler argues that, rather than the possession of some property or characteristic making a text literature, "literature" is a construction of conventions of writing and reading. A text is literature when its writer(s) and reader(s) utilize literary conventions such as "the rule of significance," according to which one reads a work "as expressing a significant attitude to some problem" that matters to humans, and "the convention of thematic unity," which entails treating the elements of a work as forwarding a theme.

As a consequence of this view, literary works must be thought of not as "harmonious totalities, autonomous natural organisms, complete in themselves and bearing a rich immanent meaning," but as utterances that have "meaning only with respect to a system of conventions which the reader has assimilated" (116). This means for Culler that theory aims not "to specify the properties of objects in a corpus," but to formulate "the internalized competence which enables objects to have the properties they do for those who have mastered the system" (120). For any literary act, such as writing a play, there is a "tacit knowledge or competence which underlies it" (123). Culler thinks literature can sustain neither an absolutism that demands that "competent readers would agree on an interpretation," nor a relativism that denies that "certain expectations about poetry and ways of reading guide the interpretive process and impose severe limitations on the set of acceptable or plausible readings" (127). Culler's notion of literary competence, like my suggestion of ethical competence, acknowledges the force of conventions without insisting that they must have a transcendent origin.

Western ethical theory has been practiced exclusively in large-scale, literate, juridically based societies, and its desire for a transcendent ethical canon reflects the tendency of such societies to externalize and make uniform: societal structure replaces individual skills whose agents are irreplaceable with functions whose agents are interchangeable. Thus a country like the United States can send humans to the moon on a rocket built by workers some of whom know how to rivet but not to wire a circuit, others of whom know how to make blueprints but not to weld, and none of whom know how to grow their own food and make their own bread. In small-scale societies, where tasks are divided differently, individual skills tend to be much more important. In a large-scale society, a function like welding can be learned in a few weekends at night school. In a small-scale society, skill at hunting is likely to be learned over years of apprenticeship. That overstates the case, no doubt, but the point is ethical rather than ethnological: ethics is not amenable to industrialization. We can organize society in such a way that someone else grows our broccoli and makes our bread, but we cannot organize society in such a way that someone else performs our ethical obligations for us. "Not I," Whitman says, "not any one else can travel that road for you, / You must travel it for yourself" (118). Lévi-Strauss's *bricolage*, introduced in *The Savage Mind*, gives a way of conceptualizing one form ethical competence can take in the absence of a transcendent canon, by treating ethical agency as a skill rather than as a function.

After a brief etymological overview, from which he concludes that in today's use, as in its old sense, "the *bricoleur* is still someone who works with his hands and uses devious means compared to those of a craftsman" (17), Lévi-Strauss gives his own definition of the term, by comparing the *bricoleur* and the engineer:

> The "bricoleur" is adept at performing a large number of diverse tasks; but, unlike the engineer, he does not subordinate each of them to the availability of raw materials and tools conceived and procured for the purpose of the project. His universe of instruments is closed and the rules of the game are always to make do with "whatever is at hand," that is to say with a set of tools and materials which is always finite and is also heterogeneous because what it contains bears no relation to the current project, or indeed to any particular project, but is the contingent result of all the occasions there have been to renew or enrich the stock or to maintain it with the remains of previous constructions or destructions. (17)

The *bricoleur* finds a way to solve the problem with the tools at hand, by adapting the available tools to the demands imposed by the problem. In doing so, the *bricoleur* applies not an overarching principle but an underlying competence.

Appropriately enough, the concept of *bricolage* is itself an adaptation of the available tools to the demands of the problem, a making something work where nothing will work. *Bricolage* must, Gayatri Spivak contends, "be placed 'under erasure'" (xx). Lévi-Strauss defines it by its opposition to "engineering," but "that opposite, a metaphysical norm, can in fact never be present and thus, strictly speaking, there is no concept of *bricolage*." The impossibility of a concept has never deterred philosophers from using it, and the impossibility of *bricolage* stops neither Lévi-Strauss nor Spivak, who admits that "the concept must be used—untenable but necessary." The idea of making do thus imposes itself, in spite of its impossibility, as one of the ways ethical agents can make do in the face of another impossibility: that of postmodernism.

Like the *bricoleur*, the ethical agent has a limited stock of tools (what I have been calling ethical canons); consequently, in ethics, the strategy of the engineer, to have a tool for every purpose (whether in the form of an unlimited supply of specialized tools or of a single tool with unlimited flexibility of purpose) will not work. The ethical agent must, like the *bricoleur*, adapt the available tools to the problem. The ethical agent must develop a skill that is not itself a rule; and the corollary is that ethical canons, like principles of chess strategy, must be applied, not correctly but skillfully.

Kathleen Marie Higgins's excellent book *The Music of Our Lives* is not concerned with postmodern theory, but in it she offers a good metaphor for an improvisational ethical methodology. Music, she says, provides "a better central model for ethics than the moral dilemma" (7):

> Mainstream ethics has largely ignored the possibility of organizing the temporal structure of one's life in such a way that its tensions do not become "moral dilemmas." Music reveals the possibility of coherent and dynamic conceptions of our ethical situation as involving problems in transition and tensions that need not necessarily be considered problems. Music, I submit, is a better model for human life.

In a *bricolage* or improvisational methodology, rather than rigidly following a single canon or substituting for ethical canons an amoral principle of decision (such as self-interest), the ethical agent can move from canon to canon not arbitrarily but in a structured way, as the Homeric bard substituted epithets according to the rhythm of the poem and the jazz musician moves freely within the limits set by the harmonic structure of the piece.

I am arguing, then, not for a new moral principle, but for a new strategy of enacting the existing ones. If ethics can be thought of as a language, as postmodern theorists suggest, then a life can be thought of as a poem. Even when we use the guidelines articulated by great ethicists like Aristotle and Kant, we use them only as poets like Seamus Heaney and Donald Justice use the strictures of sonnet form inherited from Petrarch and Shakespeare: as a space in which to create their own works. Poets know not only to follow the rules but also to change them. "If art teaches men anything, it is to become like art: not like other men" (Brodsky 273). A poet must know the rules, but must also, in the end, become a rule.

I have tried to suggest that postmodern culture demands of us, and postmodern theory advises us, to abandon the search for a single transcendent canon, and become ethical creators. Although the obligation to become a poet of the ethical is not itself a transcendent canon, and does not limit, regulate, or prescribe after the manner of canons, it is not merely a lazy relativism or nihilism. In fact, it is the most demanding ethical obligation of all, one to which postmodern theory draws attention, but which we should have known to follow all along: not only to discover the good, but to create it; not only to wish for the good, but to become it.

2. Virtuality

Whatever his other errors and exaggerations, in this Nietzsche is right: "We have *created* the world that possesses values!" (1968b:326). We have created it and programed it and strapped it on, and now we see what it shows us and we do what it demands. The world of virtue is a reality, but it is a virtual reality, one of those worlds "of poetry indistinguishable from the world in which we live" that Wallace Stevens calls "supreme fictions" (1942:31).

Ethics as Fiction

The etymology of *person* has led to widespread recognition among philosophers of the dramatic or fictional nature of personhood.

Hobbes, for instance, appeals to that etymology as justification for his definition of persons: *persona* in Latin "signifies the *disguise, or outward appearance* of a man, counterfeited on the Stage. . . . So that a *Person*, is the same that an *Actor* is, both on the Stage and in common Conversation; and to *Personate*, is to *Act*, or *Represent* himselfe, or an other" (217). However, even though ethics tries to govern or describe the interactions of (fictional) persons, philosophers have persistently repressed its fictionality. Hobbes, after producing all the necessary premises about the fictionality of persons, leaves the conclusion about the fictionality of ethics unstated. He takes pains to argue that, although human actions may be performed with liberty, which he defines as "the absence of externall Impediments" (189), yet each action also "proceedeth from some cause, and that from another cause, which causes in a continuall chaine . . . proceed from *necessity*" (263). Human actions, in other words, are determined: a human cannot initiate a causal sequence. Further, Hobbes contends that humans act on the basis of deliberation, which he defines as "the whole summe of Desires, Aversions, Hopes and Fears, continued till the thing be either done, or thought impossible" (127). Emphasis should fall on the word *thought*. We cannot deliberate about things past, since they are "manifestly impossible to be changed," nor can we deliberate about things known or thought to be impossible, but we *can* deliberate about things that we (often mistakenly) think are possible. In other words, the realm of ethics is not (to use a false dilemma) reality, but the imagination. Given those claims, humans can be morally responsible not for what we are free to do (since, all our actions being necessary, that is nothing) but for what we *imagine* ourselves free to do or what we *act as if* we are free to do. Yet Hobbes, perfectly happy to acknowledge the fictionality of persons, leaves this conclusion about the fictionality of ethics unstated, even after having stated all the premises from which this conclusion follows.

Hobbes is not alone: Western philosophy consistently has taken too little account of the fictionality of ethics. Ethical theory has displayed the deficiency Uta Frith, citing her colleague Alan M. Leslie, describes as characteristic of autism, an inability "to form and use what we might call second-order representations" (112), which Frith defines by this example:

Suppose a normal child, Beth, sees her mother holding a banana in such a way as to be pretending that it is a telephone. Beth has in mind facts about bananas and facts about telephones—first-order representations. Nevertheless, Beth is not the least bit confused and will not start eating telephones or talking to bananas. Confusion is avoided because Beth computes from the concept of pretending (a second-order representation) that her mother is engaging simultaneously in an imaginary activity and a real one. (113)

Autistic children, physiologically deprived of the ability to cognize second-order representations, lose not the reality but the fiction. Ethical theory can hardly share the physiological origin of the inability, but it has displayed similar symptoms in its refusal to recognize fictionality. Like Job's falling for God's *ad bauculum*, this ethical failure results from a failure of the imagination. The inability to enter a fictional world can separate one from the real world.

Philosophers keep trying to subsume under the category of logos—to represent as "real" and "true"—what is and always has been mythos. Not that the narrative element was invisible: from Plato's dramatic portrayals of Socrates to Nietzsche's Zarathustra and the personae of Kierkegaard to the novels of Sartre and Camus to the fiction of contemporary thinkers like William Gass, Iris Murdoch, and Lynne McFall, philosophers preoccupied with morality have turned with striking frequency to explicitly narrative forms of expression. Narrative has never been invisible in ethics, only treated as if its recurrence were an accidental feature of some discourse about ethics rather than an essential feature of ethics itself. By recognizing the inseparability of discourse from the object of discourse (or in other words of signifier from signified), postmodern theory provides an occasion for addressing fictionality in ethics.

By the fictionality of ethics I mean the quality that demands the dramatic ability to which Aristotle appeals when he says that we acquire a virtue by pretending to have it, and the act of imagination Rawls appeals to when he says that "the perspective of eternity is not a perspective from a certain place beyond the world, nor the point of view of a transcendent being; rather it is a certain form of thought and feeling that rational persons can *adopt* within the world" (587; my italics). I mean the quality of ethics that demands the capacity Yeats puts in this way:

> I think all happiness depends on the energy to assume the mask of some other life, on a re-birth as something not one's self,

something created in a moment and perpetually renewed. . . . If we cannot imagine ourselves as different from what we are, and try to assume that second self, we cannot impose a discipline upon ourselves though we may accept one from others. Active virtue, as distinguished from the passive acceptance of a code, is therefore theatrical, consciously dramatic, the wearing of a mask. (334)

In Kant one must imagine a fictional "kingdom of ends" in which one acts "*as if* the maxim of your action were to become through your will a universal law of nature" (30; my italics); in Nietzsche "one has to have a powerful imagination if one is to feel sympathy" (1986:42). And so on.

At the risk of leaving myself open to the charge leveled against epistemology in a poem by Richard Wilbur—namely, milking "the cow of the world" while whispering to it "You are not true"—I leave to one side the metaphysical consequences of fictionality. I offer as my only defense for hypothesizing the fictionality of ethics a pragmatic justification modeled on Kant's justification (in the Preface to the Second Edition of the *First Critique*) of his hypothesis that "objects must conform to our knowledge" (22). Hitherto it has been assumed that the ethical world is real. But all attempts to ground our ethical theories by discovering a transcendental principle have, on this assumption, ended in failure. We must therefore make trial whether we may not have more success in the tasks of ethics, if we suppose that the ethical world is fictional. The ethical world loses none of its weight for being fictional; it is more important than a "real" ethical world would be, for the same reason Aristotle says poetry is more important than history—namely, that it concerns "a kind of thing that might be" rather than merely what has been (1941:1451b). Ethics is not primarily a metaphysical issue but a semiological one; it is not a kind of entity but a kind of meaning.

In the chapter "Five Modes of Creation" in my book on authorship, I argued that an individual's or a culture's understanding of the process of literary creation arises in part from the type of narrative in which the poet is portrayed as the protagonist. Here I am asserting that an individual's or a culture's understanding of ethics arises in part from the genre of the narrative in which the ethical agent is portrayed as the protagonist. Thus, to initiate a major shift in ethical thought, a philosopher will change the genre of the paradigmatic ethical narrative. For example, Plato helped bring about one of the most visible of cultural shifts by telling a new kind of ethical story. In place of the bravery of the epic *Iliad*, which lets Achilles die without losing his honor, Plato posits the bravery of the tragic *Phaedo*, which lets Socrates die without losing his integrity. In place of the wisdom of Odysseus, who deceives others so that he can control them, Plato posits the wisdom of Socrates, who undeceives others so that they can control themselves. Plato helped change the ethics of a people, but he did so (in spite of all his protestations about poetry) by telling a new tale, not merely by proposing new precepts.

I have used the ethical theories of Aristotle, Kant, Mill, and Nietzsche as typical ethical canons in Western philosophy. But these same theories can also be used to illustrate the fictionality of ethics by their close relationship to literary genres. The kind of justification offered by each theory displays characteristics of a particular genre: Aristotle offers tragic justifications, Kant epic, Mill comic, and Nietzsche lyric. I will argue in this section that postmodern theory moves toward the new ethics demanded by the events of the last century, by placing justifications in a new "genre."

Tragedy

Aristotle had enough interest in tragedy to write a treatise largely devoted to it, in which he explicitly recognized the connection between literature and ethics, observing near the treatise's beginning that "the objects the imitator represents are actions, with agents who are necessarily either good men or bad" (1941:1448a). I am concerned here, though, with an *implicit* connection.

Tragedy is characterized by the protagonist's occupying a position between society and the superhuman. As Northrop Frye puts it, "The tragic hero is very great as compared with us, but there is something else, something on the side of him opposite the audience, compared to which he is small. This something else may be called God, gods, fate, accident, fortune, necessity, circumstance, or any combination of these, but whatever it is the tragic hero is our mediator with it" (207). Tragedy exemplifies Frye's "high mimetic mode," in which the protagonist is "superior in degree to other men but not to his natural environment," a person who "has authority, passions, and powers of expression far greater than ours," but who "is subject both to social criticism and to the order of nature" (33–34).

In Aristotle's own words, tragedy "is an imitation of personages better than the ordinary man" (1454b). Because of the protagonist's position, she is (or becomes) isolated from society.

Aristotle's ethical standard is, as he describes tragedy, cathartic. Tragedy purges us of pity and fear, emotions that unpurged would be harmful, and virtue in the form of habit purges us of unhealthy desires. Similarly, as tragedy orders actions into beginning, middle, and end, virtue orders volitions into deficiency, mean, and excess. Imitation operates in both, the virtuous person imitating the virtue in order to acquire it, just as the actor imitates the actions of the hero. Numerous other analogies between tragedy and Aristotle's ethics can be found in standard works like those by Kaufmann and Nussbaum, but the role of the protagonist is the most important here.

One might object to a comparison with tragedy on the grounds that in his ethics Aristotle not only asserts that happiness is the highest good, but also defines happiness as the soul's expression of complete virtue; and because tragedy ends in unhappiness, the tragic protagonist and the ethical agent are therefore disanalogous. But as Frye carefully points out, tragedy is not confined "to actions that end in disaster": tragedy can "end in serenity, like *Cymbeline*, or even joy, like *Alcestis* or Racine's *Esther*, or in an ambiguous mood that is hard to define, like *Philoctetes*." Aristotle himself points out that not the mood but the mythos is "the source of tragic effect" (1941:207). In fact, happiness is one of the points of connection between tragedy and Aristotle's ethical view. Aristotle devotes what students often consider inordinate attention to the question whether a person can be considered happy prior to death. The degree of attention Aristotle gives the question is warranted, though, if the ethical agent is a person like the tragic protagonist, in the same kind of narrative, and therefore subject to the same *peripateiai*. Like the tragic protagonist, the ethical agent aims for a happiness that is "enduring and definitely not prone to fluctuate" (1100b).

The tragic protagonist's having a *hamartia* or tragic flaw is another apparent disanalogy that is really a connection. Tragedy illustrates what happens when a person almost succeeds in being virtuous, and Aristotle in his ethics hypothesizes what would happen if a person did succeed in being virtuous. In both cases, happiness is the expression of complete virtue, and in both cases, virtue is interwoven with good or bad fortune.

Aristotle emphasizes that the protagonist in an ethical narrative, like the protagonist in a tragic narrative, can be only a particular type of person. Sometimes his clarity takes the form of explicit statement, sometimes the form of an underlying assumption. He explicitly states that animals, not being human, cannot engage in activities of the soul expressing virtue, and so can be neither virtuous nor happy (1099b). Children, not being adults, similarly are incapable of "doing these sorts of actions" (1100a). He explicitly eliminates those without the "external goods" he considers requisite for "fine actions": "we do not altogether have the character of happiness if we look utterly repulsive or are ill-born, solitary or childless" (1099b).

One of his clearest underlying assumptions insists that the protagonist of an ethical narrative be not only an adult and a human, but male. Like the rest of his society, Aristotle viewed men as by nature active, and women as by nature passive. In a household or in a city, men should rule and women should be ruled. As Foucault points out, sexual relations and social relations alike are "always conceived in terms of the model act of penetration, assuming a polarity that opposed activity and passivity." They are always between "a superior and a subordinate, an individual who dominates and one who is dominated, one who commands and one who complies, one who vanquishes and one who is vanquished" (1990b:215). Thus, Aristotle's ideal of moderation is, according to Foucault, "a man's virtue," a way "of being a man with respect to oneself; that is, a way of commanding what needed commanding, of coercing what was not capable of self-direction, of imposing principles of reason on what was wanting in reason; in short, it was a way of being active in relation to what was by nature passive and ought to remain so" (82-83).

The same assumption that makes moderation "masculine" makes it into the site of a narrative of struggle analogous to the plot of a tragedy. "What one must aim for in the agonistic contest with oneself and in the struggle to control the desires was the point where the relationship with oneself would become isomorphic with the relationship of domination, hierarchy, and authority that one expected, as a man, a free man, to establish over his inferiors" (83). In those tragedies where a woman is the protagonist, as in *Medea*, her tragic flaw is "masculinity": becoming active when she should be passive, and therefore being heteromorphic with the relationship of domination sanctioned by nature.

The ethical agent is for Aristotle, like the protagonist in tragedy, "bigger" than most humans but "smaller" than the gods. Women, children, and slaves can no more be virtuous than they can be the heroes of a tragedy, according to Aristotle. No one wrote tragedies about Briseis or the slave killed by Euthyphro's father: they were not, by the criteria of tragedy, interesting enough. Conflicts involving the weak are trivial. Only conflicts with the gods merit portrayal: "he who struggled with God," Kierkegaard says, "became greater than all" (1983:16). Similarly, Aristotle manages interest only in the few literate, property-owning males, more powerful than most of humanity, and therefore the only ones in his society powerful enough to have conflicts with each other and with the gods.

Epic

The communal function of epic gives its poet and its protagonist each a distinctive position. The epic protagonist may be, like the tragic protagonist, greater than others in society and less than the gods, but the epic protagonist is, to a degree not shared by any other dramatic entity, *representative*, a feature that leads Frye to describe the epic hero, and by extension the epic poet, as a "social spokesman" (54). The representativeness of the protagonist gives epic an objectivity well illustrated by the frequent observation that Satan, no less than God, can be read as the hero of *Paradise Lost*, and by Frye's claim that because of its recognition that the fall of even an enemy is tragic the *Iliad* bequeathed to literature "an objective and disinterested element" (319).

Because epic is encyclopedic or conservative, "the men who act in it must be," according to Eric Havelock, "the kind of men whose actions would involve the public law and the family law of the group." They must be "men whose acts, passions, and thoughts will affect the behaviour and the fate of the society in which they live so that the things they do will send out vibrations into the farthest confines of this society, and the whole apparatus becomes alive and performs motions which are paradigmatic" (167-68). Their function as paradigms often results in their becoming eponymous or assuming religious significance, like the biblical patriarchs.

Kant constructs an epic scaffolding for his ethical theory. If Aristotle's ethical protagonist resembles a tragic protagonist in being "bigger" than most people but "smaller" than nature and the gods,

Kant's ethical protagonist resembles an epic protagonist in being representative, as his formulations of the categorical imperative and his envisioning a "kingdom of ends" show. If Aristotle's ethical agent is a paragon, Kant's is a paradigm.

In his formulations of the categorical imperative, the representativeness of the ethical agent takes the form for Kant of an obligation to universality. So the first three formulations are: "I should never act except in such a way that I can also will that my maxim should become a universal law" (1981:14), "act only according to that maxim whereby you can at the same time will that it should become a universal law," and "act as if the maxim of your action were to become through your will a universal law of nature" (30). Act, in other words, as if you were an epic protagonist, whose deeds function as a paradigm.

Kant wants to make us "stock" or "cardboard" characters. When Hector takes leave of Andromache on his way to battle in book 6 of the *Iliad*, Homer does not depict them as unique individuals, but as types. Andromache gives only representative appeals for Hector to stay: you will be making your son an orphan and me a widow; and Achilles already killed my father, do not let him kill you. She offers nothing strictly "personal": she does not beg Hector to stay because she likes the way he licks the mole behind her left ear when they make love or because she likes the way his ears get red when he is angry. Indeed the fact of her appealing is itself representative: it is just what a wife should do. Similarly, Hector gives a representative reply: I am brave; and I am thinking of you. Richard Lovelace's Lucasta hears the same story a few centuries later: "I could not love thee, dear, so much / Loved I not honor more." Hector and Andromache are stock characters because they are not themselves so much as they are the Hero and the Wife. Kant's ethical protagonist is a stock character in the same way: one who acts less as a unique individual subject to the vagaries of individual desires, and therefore only capable of following hypothetical imperatives, than as a representative, as the Ethical Agent, the one who does what Anyone should.

The "kingdom of ends" reveals the epic representativeness of Kant's ethical protagonist even more clearly. He defines a kingdom of ends as "a systematic union of rational beings through common objective laws" such that each of those rational beings "should treat himself and all others never merely as a means but always at the same time as an end in himself" (1981:39). This imagined kingdom allows Kant to formulate this imperative: "A rational being must always regard himself as legislator in a kingdom of ends rendered possible by freedom of the will" (40). We are obliged as ethical agents, in other words, to act like epic protagonists. We must act in such a way that we exemplify the race, in this case the race of rational beings.

Kant is mistaken in his belief that he has identified an ethical criterion existing independently of and prior to the agent. Just as the hero of an epic becomes heroic not by meeting some independently existing criterion, but by the fact that, as members of the same culture, he shares the discursive premises of the audience—because in other words the identity of protagonist and audience derive from the same source—so Kant's ethical agent follows not an independently existing criterion, but the discursive premises of the audience. That the legislation imposed on the kingdom of ends "must be found in every rational being" does not mean that the legislation must apply to a predefined group, but that it participates in defining the group to which epic protagonist and audience belong, and that insofar as it succeeds, it makes the legislator, like the hero, representative of the group.

Comedy

In contrast to tragedy, which isolates the protagonist from society, comedy integrates society by "incorporating a central character into it" (Frye 43). The comedy may be high mimetic, low mimetic, or ironic, but in any case its protagonists will be accepted into a society from which they were previously excluded. Thus, in contrast to tragedy's focus on the protagonist, comedy "tends to deal with characters in a social group" (207), and to show not only the group's adoption of a character, but also the character's adoption of the point of view of the group in place of a self-centered point of view. This difference of emphasis reveals itself in even the most superficial ways: for example, each of Shakespeare's tragedies has as its title the proper name of its protagonist(s), yet none of his comedies do.

Mill's *Utilitarianism* offers a comic ethical narrative. Mill's ethical society, like the new society constructed at the end of a comedy, is inclusive, and the members of that new society, like the members of a comedy's new society, attune themselves to interests of the society as a whole. Utility seeks to increase happiness, but it does so, Mill carefully points out, on a global rather than an individual scale. The standard, he says, "is not the agent's own greatest happiness, but the greatest amount of happiness altogether" (11). He goes on to describe the readiness to sacrifice one's own happiness for the happiness of others as "the highest virtue which can be found" in human beings. Everyone counts in Mill's system, and everyone counts equally. "The happiness which forms the utilitarian standard of what is right in conduct is not the agent's own happiness but that of all concerned. As between his own happiness and that of others, utilitarianism requires him to be as strictly impartial as a disinterested and benevolent spectator."

Even so dark and nearly tragic a comedy as Shakespeare's *Measure for Measure* follows the pattern of inclusion Mill adopts for his ethical view. From a deputy willing to use his power to blackmail and sexually abuse the object of his ardor at the cost of violating society's interest as embodied in the law, Angelo is transformed, albeit by force, into a member of society who recognizes the value of others' interests and accedes to the regulation of his desires by the socially constructed institution of marriage. From a self-righteous prude who values her own purity over her brother's life, Isabella is transformed into a member of society able to perform the strictly social act of forgiveness. The same agents who in a tragedy would be expelled from society are in a comedy incorporated into society, and their acquiescence in engaging their social nature at the expense of their solitary nature renews the society. Mill's principle of utility is comic because it accords with "the deeply rooted conception which every individual even now has of himself as a social being," and enacts in each individual the desire for "harmony between his feelings and aims and those of his fellow creatures" (33).

Lyric

One might expect Nietzsche to exemplify the tragic genre, since he, like Aristotle, wrote a treatise on tragedy. But *The Birth of Tragedy* reflects Nietzsche's ethical genre not in its topic but in its manner of approaching the topic: it treats tragedy as lyric. Thus as his first problem he attempts to discover "how the 'lyrist' is possible as an artist—he who, according to the experience of all ages, is continually saying 'I' and running through the entire chromatic scale of his passions and desires" (1968c:48). Even in his later 'self-criticism,' attached as a preface to the 1886 edition, his primary regret about

The Birth of Tragedy is that he himself was at the time of the book's composition insufficiently lyrical.

According to Frye, if in epic the poet is, like the protagonist, a social spokesperson, in lyric the poet *is* the protagonist, an "isolated individual" whose work emphasizes "the separateness of his personality and the distinctness of his vision" (54). Although Daniel Albright calls lyric a mode rather than a genre, he too sees lyric as characterized by the poet-protagonist's role: "the writer of lyrics will tend to feel backward in his own sensibility toward a primal poet, toward a consciousness more synthetic and indiscriminate than his own, toward something almost prehuman, whom I shall call the bard" (55). Unlike the epic hero who stands for the race, the lyric bard stands against the race as a prophet, separate and filled with secret knowledge.

Proof texts to show that Nietzsche's ethical hero shares those characteristics with the lyrical bard abound. *Beyond Good and Evil* alone contains too many to reproduce: "Flee into concealment. And have your masks and subtlety, that you may be mistaken for what you are not, or feared a little" (226). "Every choice human being strives instinctively for a citadel and a secrecy where he is saved from the crowd, the many, the great majority" (227). "Our highest insights must—and should—sound like follies and sometimes like crimes when they are heard without permission by those who are not predisposed and predestined for them" (232). Et cetera.

The lyric poet's (and the lyric ethical agent's) separateness results in his consumption by the rest of society. Albright says, "The bard is consumed by the world he seeks to embrace" (59). Nietzsche says, "In solitude the solitary man consumes himself, in the crowd the crowd consumes him. Now choose" (1986:291). Nowhere is this consumption more vividly portrayed than in Yeats's play *The King's Threshold*, in which the bard Seanchan starves himself at the king's door. In that play, Yeats manages to "affirm with Shelley that the poets are the unacknowledged legislators of mankind" (Ellmann 60), but only by showing that the poet legislates not by consuming but by being consumed.

There are other correlations to be found in Albright, like that between his claim that poets "find the ideal lyric subject to be an infant touching with wonder an infantile world" (95) and Nietzsche's portrayal in *Zarathustra* of the child as the final and highest of the three metamorphoses of the spirit. And there are other versions of "lyric" to which one could compare Nietzsche, especially the rich conception articulated by Jan Zwicky, which shares with Nietzsche the ideals of clarity, passion, and resonance. Her lyrical method of juxtaposition would result in comparisons like the following. Zwicky: "Lyric is an attempt to comprehend the whole in a single gesture" (134). Nietzsche: "Half-knowledge is more victorious than whole knowledge: it understands things as being more simple than they are and this renders it opinions more easily intelligible and more convincing" (1986:188). But there is no need to push the analogy. The basic point is straightforward: lyric is characterized by the poet/protagonist's role as an inscrutable figure isolated from society, and Nietzsche casts the ethical agent in precisely such a role.

A Postmodern Acknowledgment of Virtuality

In the process of making a point about the legitimation process for scientific knowledge, Lyotard in *The Postmodern Condition* describes the necessity of what I have been calling the virtuality or fictionality of ethics. Among the points of contrast between "the pragmatics of scientific knowledge to that of narrative knowledge" (1984:25), Lyotard notes these three.

First, "scientific knowledge requires that one language game, denotation, be retained and all others excluded. A statement's truth-value is the criterion determining its acceptability." Science can accommodate "fictional" uses of language like hyperbole or metaphor only as "turning points in the dialectical argumentation, which must end in a denotative statement," or in other words, only when those language uses are controlled by the denotative uses. In contrast, narrative knowledge, which for Lyotard includes all the knowledge that "constitutes the social bond" (21), can include within itself any language game. Ethical knowledge is not, like knowledge of metabolic processes or quarks, restricted by the language game of denotation. It is fictional.

Second, "scientific knowledge is in this way set apart from the language games that combine to form the social bond. Unlike narrative knowledge, it is no longer a direct and shared component of the bond." Insofar as it is not fictional, in other words, scientific knowledge is also not ethical.

Third, "within the bounds of the game of research, the competence required concerns the post of sender alone," and consequently in the research game, "in contrast to the narrative game, a person does not have to know how to be what knowledge says he is" (26).

Narrative knowledge entails an identification and transference unavailable to scientific knowledge, and on that identification and transference ethical knowledge depends, so on Lyotard's view one should not try to make ethics "analytical" or "logical." Ethics is and must be mythos, not logos. Ethics is virtual, not "real." Ethics is fictional.

Similarly, Baudrillard has tried to address fictionality with his concept of "simulation." Appealing to "the Borges tale where the cartographers of the Empire draw up a map so detailed that it ends up exactly covering the territory," Baudrillard argues that "simulation is no longer that of a territory, a referential being or a substance. It is the generation by models of a real without origin or reality: a hyperreal. The territory no longer precedes the map, nor survives it. Henceforth, it is the map that precedes the territory—PRECESSION OF SIMU-LACRA—it is the map that engenders the territory" (1983b:1-2). He claims that the difference between the real and the imaginary has disappeared. If Nietzsche proclaimed the death of god and Barthes the death of the author, Baudrillard proclaims the death of representation. Representation tries to bring the real into the symbolic order, on the assumption that the symbolic order has value to the degree to which it conveys the real. But when the difference between real and symbolic disappears, the real disappears with it; so "the real is no longer real" (25), but is always already subsumed by simulation.

That ethics *is* not matter does not mean that it *does* not matter, as Baudrillard carefully points out. The disappearance of the real does not eliminate danger, since the symbolic, as we of the literati should know, was every bit as powerful as the real even before the real disappeared. "A war," Baudrillard says, "is not any the less heinous for being a mere simulacrum—the flesh suffers just the same, and the dead ex-combatants count as much there as in other wars" (70). Like Southern Baptists chafing against the use of the word *myth* by theologians to refer to biblical narratives, philosophers have repressed the fictionality of ethics by acting as if "fictional" entailed "false," but the significance of the ethical is not diminished by the realization that it is virtual rather than real.

Intertextuality in Place of Genre

Postmodern theory does not explicitly propose a change in the genre of ethical discourse any more than previous ethicists explicitly proposed such a change. But even without being conscious of doing so,

Kant "used" a different genre than did Aristotle, and Mill a different genre than did Kant. Similarly, I believe that postmodern theory has relied, without intending to, on a "genre" it has named "intertextuality."

The genres in which earlier ethicists have constructed their theories assume a clear identity for the protagonist, and a clear distinction between active and passive. In regard to texts, however, postmodern theory draws into question both of those assumptions, and by acknowledging the fictionality of ethics poses the same problem for the ethical agent. The protagonist of a narrative is no longer a simple entity separate from author and reader, nor is the author or reader a simple entity separate from the other. Each is in part composed by the others, and by the texts in which they participate.

Julia Kristeva coined the term *intertextuality* to designate a concept that she finds in Bakhtin, that she contends "replaces that of intersubjectivity," and that she explains in this way: "any text is constructed as a mosaic of quotations; any text is the absorption and transformation of another" (1980:66). Worton and Still give two reasons why a text "cannot exist as a hermetic or self-sufficient whole, and so does not function as a closed system":

> Firstly, the writer is a reader of texts (in the broadest sense) before s/he is a creator of texts, and therefore the work of art is inevitably shot through with references, quotations and influences of every kind. . . . Secondly, a text is available only through some process of reading; what is produced at the moment of reading is due to the cross-fertilisation of the packaged textual material (say, a book) by all the texts which the reader brings to it. (1-2)

Just as biology has begun to question the individuality of individuals, preferring descriptions of human individuals as concatenations of symbiotic microbes that are themselves inseparable from the other microbes with which they freely exchange genetic material, or from the "planetary patina" they compose, so postmodern theory questions the individuality of individuals, whether authors, readers, or ethical agents, preferring descriptions that do not artificially extricate them from the various matrices they compose and are composed by.

The "genre" of intertextuality frames an ethic no less than the genre of tragedy or lyric, but it is an ethic "after experience," which, as Kristeva puts it, renounces the coercion of a group into cohesiveness "through the repetition of a code," and replaces it with "the free play of negativity, need, desire, pleasure, and jouissance" (23), or in other words stops trying to extricate the code from the matrices it composes and is composed by. Kristeva's program for "the ethics of linguistics" closely resembles the "postmodern virtue" I am advocating. Kristeva's linguistic ethics "would deflect linguistics toward a consideration of language as an articulation of a heterogeneous process" (24), as postmodern theory asks us to consider ethics as a heterogeneous process that precludes the hegemony of a single principle. Kristeva advocates establishing "*poetic language* as the object of linguistics' attention in its pursuit of truth in language" (25), as I advocate the use of poiesis (in the broad etymological sense that includes poetry along with other creative arts like music) as a model for virtue.

Poetic language is important for Kristeva because it cannot be accounted for by "any logical system based on a zero-one sequence (true-false, nothingness-notation)" (70). Poetic language calls for "the 0-2 interval," a dialogic "dream logic" that escapes the social prohibition of the "1 (God, Law, Definition)" by "*analogy* and *nonexclusive opposition*" instead of "monologic levels of causality and identifying determination" (72). The resulting "carnivalesque structure" is "composed of distances, relationships, analogies, and nonexclusive oppositions," in which "two texts meet, contradict, and relativize each other" (78). Kristeva takes intertextuality to imply that philosophical problems occur "*within* language; more precisely, within language as a correlation of texts, as a reading-writing that falls in with non-Aristotelian, syntagmatic, correlational, "carnivalesque" logic. Consequently, one of the fundamental problems facing contemporary semiotics is precisely to describe this "other logic" without denaturing it" (89). Ethics, insofar as it is semiological, faces the same problem.

The problem is that the subject has been fragmented into "multiple doers," so the subject's discourse or the subject's ethical activity "inscribes, not the original-paternal law, but other laws that can enunciate themselves differently beginning with these pronominal, transsubstantive agencies. Its legitimacy is illegal, paradoxal, heteronymic; heteronomous in relation to Hegelian Law, it struggles with constancy and originality" (113). The subject is not a tabula rasa on which the white right hand of God writes its law, but a palimpsest graffitied in the pidgins of a thousand passersby.

Aristotle's rational animal and Descartes' thinking being died not long after Adam the image of God; whatever story postmodern virtue tells will be a collage, not a sculpture, and will be, like its protagonists, composite, multiple, and heterogeneous. Postmodern theory does to genre what it does to canons: it points out the impossibility of our finding or maintaining a "pure" and self-contained ethic.

3. Virtuosity

Ethical ideals are various, but their variety can be ordered into an array determined by specific variables. One of those variables, agency vs. activity, is widely recognized: ethicists regularly divide theories according to whether they are act-centered or agent-centered. But I propose two others, the temporal variable of past vs. future and the spatial variable of internal vs. external. With the requisite disclaimer that no one of these variables exists by itself (an ideal cannot be wholly agent-centered, to the complete exclusion of weighing actions), an ethical ideal will result from the conjunction of two of these variables. For instance, by privileging activity and externality, or in other words by concerning oneself primarily with what is done rather than with who did it, and with how the action affects what is external to it rather than with what the action is in itself or how it stands in relation to the agent who performed it, one arrives at an ideal of efficacy. The entire array of possibilities looks like this:

		Past	*Future*
Time	*Agency*	archeology	eschatology
	Activity	revision	construction
Space	*Agency*	singularity	solidarity
	Activity	integrity	efficacy
		Internal	*External*

Ethical ideals differ from ethical canons, in that the latter are the means by which to tell whether one has attained the former. One follows a canon or canons in order to fulfill an ideal.

Temporal Ideals

The ideal I am calling archæology attempts to preserve the past. E. M. Cioran appeals to this ideal when he says:

> The quest for beginnings is the most important of all those we can undertake. Each of us makes it, if only in brief moments, as if performing this return presented the unique means of recovering and transcending ourselves, of triumphing over ourselves and over everything. It is also the only mode of escape that is not a desertion or a deception. But we have got in the habit of attaching ourselves to the future, of putting apocalypse above cosmogony, of idolizing the explosion and the end, of banking to an absurd degree on the Revolution or the Last Judgment. Would it not be wiser to turn back, toward a chaos much richer than the one we anticipate? (207-8)

Political views labeled "conservative" embody the ideal of archæology, as do modern judicial systems based on precedent and constitutional political systems.

Political views labeled "liberal" embody the ideal I am calling eschatology, which attempts to produce a future unlike any previous time. A call to revolution pursues this ideal, so Marx exemplifies a preoccupation with this ideal. The communist revolution he envisaged would produce, he thought, a society without classes and therefore without conflict, a society in which participants in government had interests identical with the governed, a society free from exploitation, in which work was always satisfying: a society, in other words, completely unlike any previous society. The ethical ideal of eschatology also motivates the modernist aesthetic imperative to "make it new."

Revision is the wish or attempt to alter the past. Unlike archæology, which wants to preserve the past into the present, revision wants to liberate the present by changing the past. No philosophical system depends more exclusively on the ideal of revision than does psychoanalysis. Freud sees the patient's life as a narrative, and the analyst as an editor. The patient has told the story of his life wrong, and the analyst must take the patient back to the flaw in the story and write/right it again. A patient is unhealthy in the present because of his past; the analyst restores the patient's health (the Freudian substitute for virtue) in the present by changing the patient's past.

Construction wants to liberate the present not by changing the past but by binding the future. Unlike eschatology, for which the present is the means to a future different from the past, in the ideal of construction the future is a means to a vital present. Contracts express the ideal of construction, and a social contract political theory like that of Hobbes is a perfect example of a philosophical view that pursues the ideal of construction. In the state of nature, according to Hobbes, life is "solitary, poore, nasty, brutish, and short" in the present, but it is so because the *future* is unbound. Life in a state of nature would be nasty, brutish, and short because it would lack industry, agriculture, navigation, building, knowledge, arts and letters, and the like, and it would lack them "because the fruit thereof is uncertain." Only by "constructing" the future through contract, according to Hobbes, can we benefit in the present. The social institution of marriage, similarly, is predicated on construction. The love of marriage partners is "true" because it is always already waiting for the partners to meet it in the future. The present, according to this ideal, can be full and happy only if the future has made its promises in writing.

Spatial Ideals

Joseph Brodsky's belief that "prison is a lot better than the army" expresses the ideal of singularity, which is the desire for originality or uniqueness. Brodsky says, "It is the army that finally makes a citizen of you; without it you still have a chance, however slim, to remain a human being. If there is any reason for pride in my past, it is that I became a convict, not a soldier" (24), that he was, in other words, a nonconformist. This is a "spatial" ideal because it locates the agent, placing him in opposition to a community. It is "internal" because any action that expresses this ideal will "come from inside" the person.

In contrast to singularity, the ideal of solidarity expresses the wish for conformity, and thus places the ethical agent within a community. It is an "external" ideal because its source will be not the individual herself, but either the community to which she belongs or something that helps found that community, like god or duty. Patriotism of any stripe will express the ideal of solidarity. Postromantic literary and philosophical examples more often oppose solidarity than praise or enact it, as in Wilfred Owen's indictment of the saying *Dulce et decorum est pro patria mori*, and W. H. Auden's ironic portrayal of "The Unknown Citizen," but earlier texts are full of examples of this ideal. Achilles is praised in the *Iliad* for his strength and courage, but criticized for holding out while the other Achæans were fighting. Socrates, for all his willingness in the *Apology* to adopt the ideal of singularity, expresses solidarity in the *Crito*.

Descartes expresses the ideal of integrity when, in his temporary moral code in the *Discourse on the Method*, he decides to "try always to conquer myself rather than fortune, and to alter my desires rather than change the order of the world" (96-97). Montaigne had adopted the same ideal a few years before, when he said that fortune can do neither good nor harm, but can only supply the soul with "the material and the seed of them" in the form of external circumstances, which the soul uses as the body uses clothes, which "keep us warm not by their heat but by our own" (46). Thus he adopted this precept: "Not being able to rule events, I rule myself, and adapt myself to them if they do not adapt themselves to me" (488). Integrity is spatial because, like singularity and duty, it uses an inside/outside framework, directing the agent inward.

In contrast to integrity, efficacy directs the agent outward, asking not how I should change in response to the world, but how I can make it change in response to me. Marx espouses this ideal when he complains that "philosophers have only interpreted the world in various ways; the point is to change it" (158), but no ideology shows a more exclusive attachment to this ideal than does behaviorism. B. F. Skinner gladly discards internal states like "personalities, states of mind, feelings, traits of character, plans, purposes, intentions, or the other perquisites of autonomous man" so long as he can "get on with a scientific analysis of behavior" that will help to "solve the terrifying problems that face us in the world today" (12-13, 1). Skinner cares not about how you are affected by what is external to you, but about what effect you have on what is external to you.

Any canon will pursue some combination of those ideals. For instance, of the temporal ideals, Mill's utilitarianism pursues construction in its evaluation of present worth by future consequences. Of the spatial ideals, it pursues solidarity by demanding a readiness to sacrifice one's own interests for that of the community to which one belongs, and efficacy by evaluating "external" rather than "internal" effects. The array of ideals provides a means for comparing ethical views, and a way of "plotting" or describing differences between similar views. For instance, the often-noted change from the teaching of Jesus to Paul can be characterized as a change in one of the temporal ideals: Jesus is depicted with some consistency by the gospels as favoring eschatology with its revolutionary implications, but Paul very consistently chooses construction, the more conservative, institutional ideal. But the array of ideals also offers a way of characterizing the ethical approach suggested by postmodern theory.

A Postmodern Approach to Ethical Ideals

Postmodern theory longs for an ideal that is not an ideal, for a metaideal that will allow the ethical agent / patient to adopt and configure other ideals. This improvisatory longing is not unique to the postmoderns. Schlegel expresses it by a musical metaphor: "A really free and cultivated person ought to be able to attune himself at will to being philosophical or philological, critical or poetical, historical or rhetorical, ancient or modern: quite arbitrarily, just as one tunes an instrument, at any time and to any degree" (7). The postmoderns prefer metaphors that move across space rather than time, but they express the same longing.

Foucault talks about matrices and lattices. Instead of being static, power and knowledge (the components for Foucault of what goes by the name of virtue) are what he calls "matrices of transformation" (1990a:99). In other words, the power relationships between humans form a field in which the locations of particular people determine their power, as the location of a particular piece in a game of chess influences its strength, knights being much more powerful in the center than on the edge of the board. Foucault's ideal is to be able, like the queen in chess, to move in virtually unrestricted fashion over the matrix.

Roland Barthes includes ethical systems, like all other systems, in the category of texts (remember *Mythologies* or *The Fashion System*) and describes writing as "the morality of form" (1968b:15). He describes texts as "multi-dimensional spaces" which are to be "ranged over, not pierced" (1977:146-47). Barthes wants to destroy duration, the crucial component of order that makes it "always a murder in intention" (1968b:39), in order to make possible his ideal, a "stretching" of the subject over the whole textual space.

Other postmoderns pursue the same ability to "range over" the array of ideals. Derrida talks about "decentering," pulling out the stake by which we are tethered to the space of a single ideal. Lévi-Strauss advocates *bricolage*, allowing the worker the entire space of the toolbox and the tool the entire space of the task. Kristeva describes the "ideologeme" as having access to all of semiotic space. Baudrillard talks of a "telematics" in which "we no longer exist as playwrights or actors but as terminals of multiple networks" (1988:16), or in which, in other words, we are no longer restricted to the single space in which "individuals" exist, but instead now roam freely over many spaces or screens. Lyotard talks at the end of *The Postmodern Condition* about "paralogy," a state in which localized language games are distributed across political space, but in which citizens can gain "perfect information" by moving with "free access" across the various language games.

Nowhere, though, does postmodern theory treat this theme more exhaustively than in Deleuze and Guattari's *A Thousand Plateaus*, the explicit purpose of which is "to make thought travel, to make it mobile" (343). Deleuze and Guattari travel across different formulations of the theme. They talk of deterritorializing and reterritorializing space, rather than coding and decoding space, or in other words of allowing the relations of movement to construct space (as in Go), rather than allowing space to constrict movement (as in Chess). The result is smooth space, for which felt, a nonhomogeneous, aggregated entanglement, is a metaphor, rather than striated space, for which woven cloth, with its separation of threads, patterned intertwining, and warp and woof, is a metaphor. They prefer the "rhizome" to "arboresence." They talk of the war machine and its nomad science, which, as illustrated by ancient atomism, "uses a hydraulic model" and "is inseparable from flows," and in which "flux is reality itself," in preference to the state apparatus and its royal science, which is "a theory of solids treating fluids as a special case" (361). Nomad science, they say, does across physical space what I am suggesting postmodern theory consistently says ethical agents do across the array of ideals: it is "distributed by turbulence across a smooth space," and produces "a movement that holds space and simultaneously affects all of its points, instead of being held by space in a local movement from one specified point to another"

(363). They talk of a "compars" method of science that "reproduces," or looks for constants, and compare it unfavorably to a "dispars" method that "follows" a "flow in a vectorial field across which singularities are scattered" (372). They argue that because "every semiotic is mixed and only functions as such," and "each one necessarily captures fragments of one or more other semiotics," there can be no "general semiology" (no totalizing ethical principle) but only a "transsemiotic" (a movement across various principles) (136).

The formulation, though, in which Deleuze and Guattari most obviously capture in their general view the specifically ethical view with which I am concerned here is their discussion of punctual vs. multilinear systems (294-98). Punctual systems organize themselves around points: lines "serve as coordinates for assigning points." Punctual systems provide fixity. Multilinear systems, in contrast, provide movement. "In a multilinear system, everything happens at once: the line breaks free of the point as origin; the diagonal breaks free of the vertical and the horizontal as coordinates; and the transversal breaks free of the diagonal as a localizable connection between two points." Punctual systems are the aim of (royal) science and the state; multilinear systems are the aim of artists and, I am suggesting, ethical agents. "Free the line, free the diagonal: every musician or painter has this intention." The artist and the ethical agent want to "send a tremor through" the punctual system, to use it as "a springboard to jump from." I appealed above to the jazz musician's improvisation as a metaphor; Deleuze and Guattari offer the classical musician as their prototype for one who knows how to range over the array. "The important thing is that all musicians have always proceeded in this way: drawing their own diagonal, however fragile, outside points, outside coordinates and localizable connections," wandering freely over the punctual system in order to create their multilinear system, "in order to float a sound block down a created, liberated line." The ethical agent, like the musician, creates and liberates, which one can never do by adherence to a canon or confinement within a punctual system.

Given an array of ideals like the one I have elaborated above, the postmodern "ideal," then, is not the selection of a single ideal from the possible choices enumerated, and a consistent adherence to it, but the ability to travel at will over the array, to select and combine ideals creatively. Traditional ethics resists and denies movement over the array of ideals, because it agrees with Kant that "consistency is the highest obligation of a philosopher" (1956:23).

Postmodern ethics embraces and affirms that movement, agreeing with Emerson's dictum that consistency is "the hobgoblin of little minds." Against the accusation of arbitrariness (you don't have a principle for selecting or combining ideals in a given situation, but do so groundlessly!), the reply is a *tu quoque*: the choice of a single ideal is also arbitrary and groundless, since a person could only choose an ideal nonarbitrarily by implementing an already (arbitrarily) chosen ideal. The insistence on retaining freedom of movement displayed by the "postmodern virtue" for which I am arguing is, as I cannot say often enough, neither an excuse for dissipating responsibility nor the guise of a lazy relativism: nothing dissipates responsibility more readily than transferring it to a rule or a ruling individual, and no one has more responsibility than the artist who is subject to no single rule.

If postmodern theory has been reticent in its ethical prescriptions, preferring to conceal them or present them in the guise of hermeneutics or science, the reticence comes from the recognition not only that imperatives are, like other speech acts, impure forms that contain their opposites in themselves—in this case, a call to violate the call to observe—but also the correlative idea that imperatives can only take a paradoxical form. Just as the one available form of wisdom is the paradoxical Socratic recognition of one's own lack of wisdom, so the one categorical imperative is not the "rational" Kantian universalization of the maxim but the paradoxical Wittgensteinian call to "transcend these propositions." The only binding ethical imperative is the imperative to transcend imperatives. Wittgenstein took this as a call to end discourse, but postmodern theory has taken it as a call to endless discourse. Wittgenstein thought that we could not talk about ethics, but postmodernism, for all its many flaws, has recognized that virtue is one thing we cannot *stop* talking about.

12 Postmodern Postscript(s)

> *I'll know no further.*
> —*Shakespeare*, Coriolanus

Postmodern Preface(s)

In the preface the writer tells what she has forgotten to say in the rest of the work; in the postscript she says what she wanted to say in the rest of the work, but could not.

A journey to a distant place should be begun at night and in secret. If those to be left behind must know about and attend the departure, their assembly should be silent.

Desire is the emptiness of repetition. Pleasure is the repetition of emptiness.

A life can only steal from the rich and give to the poor. A work can add to the available wealth.

Virtuous texts make promises: "Blessed is he that readeth, and they that hear the words of this prophecy, and keep those things that are written therein." A vicious text would offer no assurances, not even the Mephistophelean promise of damnation (which is only, after all, the bliss of the guilty).

Some authors write many books, some write the same book many times, and some write a number of books that become one book.

Once composition was the serious task, and reading was "play"; now that composition is a game, reading has assumed the gravity that once belonged to writing.

Writing is not self-disclosure, but self-enclosure: to conceal oneself in beautiful or exemplary ways.

Most writers write only books they have read, and most readers read only books they would write were they able.

Wisdom reads what it would not write, genius writes what it has not read.

Read 1,000 books. Befriend 100. Know 10 by heart. Write 1.

Most readers treat texts as astrologers treat stars, insisting that they tell us something we do not already know.

A book must have a market, and even the avant-garde must have a name. No longer do we merely ignore the voice crying in the wilderness, now we try systematically to eliminate the possibility of its being heard.

———————

One song is as good as another only when one ear is as good as another.

———————

One reads what one is prepared to understand, but that is so little that one's mind soon begins to close in on itself. If it is impossible to know everything, it is also contemptible to withdraw into the knowledge of only one thing.

———————

Every mind has its own particular temptations and failures, but inertia is a universal threat: to move in only one direction at only one speed.

———————

Knowledge does not always change what a person will do or experience, but it always changes why one does what one does and how one experiences what one experiences.

———————

Ideas do not come to one at the end of long chains of reasoning, but with the suddenness of violent impact. The force of the impact lasts, not the idea itself, and not the reasoning that follows after.

———————

Like a gas, like language, god expands to fill the space provided.

———————

So that its history would be consistent with its theology, Christianity, like its founder, had to die.

Postmodern Grief

A lament is always the mask of a different lament hidden behind it.

Suicides often send out warning signals of their despair. So do the good, the visibly healthy, the well adjusted.

Suicide: a successful revolution against the tyranny of despair. Happiness: a tyranny so complete that the reigning despair is not even threatened by revolt.

The impulse toward self-destruction need not take the form of suicide. One who could not even conceive of ending his life may try hard to ruin it.

That retreat alone makes it possible shows that thought is a form of self-preservation.

A prophet cannot endure good news.

Success can be measured not by the duration of one's survival but by the alterity of one's death. Success is not to perpetuate the species, but to die as an individual.

Death admits of differences only in quality, not in degree. The dead do not get more dead, but they do get better at it.

It is wrong to run from death, wrong to run to it, and foolish to ignore it. All that remains is to embrace it when it arrives.

Holding the mirror up to nature is more interesting than holding it up to oneself. That nature is nothing is always news; that one is oneself nothing is never news to anyone but oneself.

Only as the story of a death can the story of a life interest us.

Postmodern Aporesis

If those with whom you live and work understand what you are doing while you are doing it, you are wasting your time.

One must leave all, and only, the messages one cannot leave.

One becomes a prophet by insisting on, and persisting in, believing in oneself, in spite of all the evidence.

A world in which God could exist would prove that there was no God; this world, in which the existence of a God is inconceivable, proves that there is a God.

That which would articulate the abyss must itself be an abyss.

If the mad are not conscious of their madness, the sane cannot be sure of their sanity. If the foolish are not conscious of their foolish-ness, the wise cannot be sure of their wisdom. Thus, although a mind can transcend other minds, it can never be certain of having done so.

———————

Truly wisdom is the highest prize to be attained by humans; unfor-tunately, one must already have wisdom in order to acquire it.

———————

Argumentation is superfluous. Not whether an idea is accepted, but whether and in what way and by whom it is entertained, matters.

———————

One invents the ideas one needs; one discovers the ideas one cannot avoid. Recognition and confrontation can only be discovered, not invented. The most compelling ideas are those one can neither believe nor forget.

———————

Silence per se is not valuable, but the conditions are under which it alone is appropriate.

———————

To understand the ideas of another would be to isolate the point at which silence becomes necessary. Wars and homicides occur because the parties have not understood each other. They stopped talking before they had to. As long as silence is merely possible, murder is possible too. Only where silence is necessary is murder impossible.

———————

Which is greater, an omnipotent God or a God that does not need to be omnipotent? Which is more advanced, a consistent God or a God who does not need to be consistent?

———————

A thousand butterflies, a dozen humans, a single angel. In a world in which rebirth was possible, they would be the same. In this world, they are merely no different.

———————

Equal distribution of leisure destroys: leisure should be reserved exclusively for those who will refuse it.

Postmodern Freedom

Independence may be unattainable, but not autonomy. One can choose on whom and for what one will depend.

———————

Those for whom nothing is necessary and from whom nothing is expected, possess the only freedom: the freedom to perish.

———————

Because we do not choose to make mistakes, they always occur with the force of necessity. Because mistakes are necessary, we can never believe in what we choose.

———————

To create a work liberates it—and oneself.

———————

History is a self-moving force because, although humans cannot change themselves, they can be changed.

———————

Some people *do* manufacture angels out of what they eat, and some, more importantly, manufacture gods.

———————

The mind capitulates not to the world but to itself. The good news is that the world cannot overcome the mind; the bad news is that it does not need to.

The world conforms to the mind of the percipient only long enough to load its gun.

Were there no windows already open on eternity, the difference in pressure would shatter the ones that are closed.

To fall on one's knees is not always the same as to be driven to them.

Although we often praise it, to persist in something futile is a damnable form of attempting the impossible: it avoids the risk of failure by making failure certain, and by choosing to fail it makes failure into success.

Postmodern Beauty

Ideas cease to function and thereby become obsolete. Passions cease to exist and thereby command lasting honor. Once an idea has engendered another idea, it becomes sterile. A passion may breed infinitely many children.

Ideas cannot produce effects at a distance; passions can.

Thought that matters is passion, passion that matters is discipline,

discipline that matters is courage, courage that matters is beauty, beauty that matters is sorrow, sorrow that matters is thought.

Young artists see their activity as a form of protest. Unfortunately, having nothing to protest, and sensing that they have neither the patience nor the discipline to acquire the skills of art, most protest art itself. Then they wonder why their work is empty, or refuse to see that it is.

Art changes the geometry of the world. It draws us to the edge where the unimagined falls off into the unimaginable.

The thinker's task: to make sense of a world. The artist's task: to make of sense a world.

That two people cannot simultaneously become the center of the universe dooms the artist to solitude. It only takes one god to make a world.

The great book or painting or musical score comes only after long labor, but never as the result of the labor. One must be prepared not only to work until one is a stranger to any pleasure other than labor, but also to discard all that one has labored on for what offers itself. One forfeits one's life for one's labor, and then one forfeits one's labor as well. One cannot earn genius, only the worthiness to receive its offerings.

The artist is the invincible person.

Could we encounter ourselves, we would do so in art. Could we encounter art, we would do so in ourselves.

Art must do what the world cannot.

A work of art can do more than change a life; it can save one.

The artist counts stars through the holes in the ceiling while falling through a hole in the floor.

The necessity that drives one person to create has a quantitative measure: how many others it impels to re-create the same thing how long afterward. Not popularity, which like a yawn prompts many imitations among its contemporaries, but imposition, which like parental violence commands replications in children and grand-children and greatgrandchildren.

Genius is a form of masochism. Everyone except the geniuses them-selves wants the pleasures that attend the public reception of genius: the applause after a piano concert, the immortality of a great novel or painting, the wealth and status of the great scien-tist. (Indeed, those things attend genius at the end of or after the genius's career because that is what others think the genius wants, and they do not—they could not—recognize genius until too late to give it what it needs.) The geniuses themselves want not the plea-sures public reception of their work offers (which in fact they often reject) but the perpetual, immeasurable pain that the private activ-ity of genius inflicts.

Inspiration: the lie genius tells to protect its secret.

Genius finds what no one but itself could will, and wills it in defiance of what everyone but itself wills.

The rest of the world looks on while a few geniuses create it.

Do geniuses know that they are geniuses? Yes. That knowledge alone enables them to survive the condition. The few geniuses who are not certain—the Van Goghs and the Berrymans—do not survive.

Genius may not show itself in, but it is earned by, the quotidian.

The timelessness of artworks once meant the perpetuation in them of the past. Now the timelessness of artworks means the production in them of a perpetual present.

As long as art is mimetic, it is loss. What art represents will always possess something art itself does not. Only art capable of presenting instead of re-presenting can add to the world instead of subtracting from it.

As long as the creation of the work is bound by chronology, so that the artist must precede it, its content is bound by chronology as well. The audience can only discover in the work the remnants of the artist. But when the creation of the work is liberated from chronology, when its audience can help create it, its content is liberated from chronology as well. The audience then can find itself.

Philosophy requires pride, the belief that one is strong enough to win others. Art requires vanity, the belief that one is beautiful enough to win others.

One reasons to stifle resistance. One makes art to defy it.

If truth is an extinct totem animal, reason specifies where it would be found if it still existed, and art describes what the animal would look like if you could get there.

Mathematician and philosopher are bound by the equation as their basic pattern. Only art (and it only in moments of transcendence) escapes the equation.

Where I find meaning I cannot find myself. Only where I create meaning can I find myself.

The writer's aim is to become an oracle: to achieve a voice so profound that its words can never be fully fathomed, so forceful that the world conforms to its will. Every sentence a riddle, every word a fate.

Force may win anything but what has force, the winning of which is reserved not for those who are victorious over it but those who have been defeated by it.

Postmodern Obscenity

If you do not have to be mystified any more, you cannot be.

Nature makes us eat and piss and shit; society insists we hold a job and buy a house and insure it and pay the bills and fix the plumbing and get the car tuned up and save for retirement and exercise and marry and beget. But the great begrudge all discourse with what is external to them and obligatory: the ordinary diverts and diminishes them. The great resent even being loved, because it is a distraction, a humiliation.

The most absurd, measly fate of all: a life of goodness.

Nothing of interest can be counted. Nothing of worth numbers more than one.

In anarchy, where every individual is a law unto herself, there are no individuals: everyone follows the same principle. Individuals can exist only in a social context that prohibits autonomy. Although few outlaws are individuals, all individuals are outlaws.

Guiltless is a synonym for trivial.

One may deserve an idea, or not deserve it.

Unnecessary words pollute.

A false asceticism directs itself against all forms of pleasure, but a more discriminating asceticism recognizes the pleasures one chooses as signs of the value one places on life, and denies itself pleasures that diminish life. Entertainment and dissipation are bad, not because they are done strictly for pleasure (since they are done for the illusion of pleasure, not being truly pleasurable at all), but because they reveal the emptiness of the individual engaged in them.

———————

Crises realize not merely years but generations or centuries of decay.

Postmodern Censorship

Even when many people are courteous to a work of art, only a few will love it.

———————

To register, to hoard, to be actively receptive, to let wisdom accumulate if it will. To have a mental life of movement and energy, not to wither into one of those thinkers—so common—who make a career out of one idea. To occupy a position that no one else has occupied, or could occupy. Not to fear being foolish. Not to fear becoming wise.

———————

Not to have a bad conscience about what I have written but no longer believe, not to try to erase or correct, not even to waste the effort of renunciation, but simply to move on.

———————

To be outside the gravitational field of sanction. To resist the temptation to seek approbation and support, and to remember if it should come always to watch it warily.

———————

Our hatred of ideas that oppose the ideas we believe in, and of persons who believe such ideas, results not from our conviction that the opposing idea is wrong, but from our envy of the person who holds the idea for possessing a capacity we do not possess.

The more one knows, the more one is capable of feeling: the ignorant are capable of only the shallowest of feelings. But the more one knows, the less one needs to feel. Profound minds alone are capable of profound feelings, and inclined to refuse them.

We fear not the unknown but the almost known.

Ill will may originate not only in resentment, the recognition in others of what one cannot have for oneself, but also in the recognition in others of what one cannot rid oneself of, since what is worst in others always also inhabits oneself.

People think all the indictments they make come from God, as dogs think all that moves is alive.

People do not know to heed the words of a prophet, but they know to fear the prophet's presence.

A person may be dishonest under any circumstances, but honest only in the face of death, when lies lose their interest. The honest are all dead or soon to be killed. This is the sense in which prophets are ahead of their time: they are not the first to whom the future appears, but the first whom death visits.

In a world of explosions, an implosion would have its own force as well as the force of all that surrounds it.

Postmodern Color

Some people want to spread their lives out over an indefinite amount of space: to see, in other words, all there is to see. Others want to spread their lives out over an indefinite amount of time: to do all there is to do.

We would first have to come to terms with the Other in order to be able to come to terms with ourselves. We would first have to come to terms with ourselves to be able to come to terms with the Other.

All humans are intolerant of the Other. "Tolerant" individuals are so because they recognize affinities between themselves and what is outside them, so the category of the Other for them is small.

The preference for strangers: one need feel no guilt, one is not killing *them.*

Self-knowledge comes less from examining the self than from examining the other; less from looking inward than from looking outward. One learns what one is by learning what one is not. One discovers what one really values, for instance, by confronting the values of another. One's real values reveal themselves when dialogue ceases, when one no longer gives reasons (either because there are no more reasons to be given or because one no longer feels compelled to give what reasons there are).

Even about suffering we are intolerant: you must suffer *my* way. Only the torments I can understand, only the torments a person like myself might suffer are permissible.

The most distant stars can be seen only when one's nearest neighbors cannot.

Ignorance is an act of revenge on all the great minds that have preceded and formed—and excelled—our own.

The automobile as the representative object of American culture: fast, expensive, excessive, lethal. The automobile wreck as the definitive event.

Utopian visions always depend on the imagined possibility of a change that is not exchange, a change that is pure gain untempered by loss.

The risks and failings of enforced inequality are enormous, and its damage immeasurable, but the same is true of attempts to enforce equality.

"The whole" is a tool for eliminating opposition, or another name for having successfully eliminated it.

The defeated long for victory; the victorious long for peace; the peaceful long for another war.

A world in which all living creatures can lie down without fear is impossible. It would be enough if each creature could distinguish what it should fear from what it need not.

Even the aim of peace we achieve by the destruction of a common enemy.

What is greatness but to learn to kill only those one chooses to kill, and to choose to kill only those who deserve to die? What is greatness but to be peaceful only on one's own terms?

We labor not to achieve peace but in youth to simulate it and in age to substitute for it.

The privileged are capable of boredom. The powerful can kill with impunity. The only relief from boredom is to witness a death. Increasingly spectacular deaths are needed to forestall boredom, so the destruction of the species is inevitable.

Civilization teaches us more subtle methods of murder. Its aim is to enable one to be the last left standing in a world without stones.

To the one who has much, more will be given; from the one who has little, all will be taken away. Civilization presents the problem of evil as if it were its own solution, as if having much always meant deserving much.

The oppressed always think they could wield power without oppressing.

―――――――

Prophecy is futile because even disaster cannot penetrate false consciousness unless it is one's own disaster.

Postmodern Love

The quality of a relationship is defined not by honesty, but by what one person cannot say to the other. Intimacy is determined by the gravity of what is proscribed. Love thus makes one more private, more solitary. One cannot permit anything that matters to escape, and over time one's density, pressure, weight increases.

―――――――

Marriage demands that one's imagination be strong enough to accommodate the imagination of one other, and no stronger.

―――――――

One knows best not those with whom one spends years but those with whom one spends seconds. Lovers and friends spend imprisoned lifetimes trying vainly to recover the knowledge they shared in the first glance, the first word. An epistemological error lies behind many of the failures of Western culture, including the institution of marriage: the conception of knowledge by analogy with familiarity instead of immediacy.

―――――――

One lover's resources determine what both lovers do. What that lover cannot do, the other lover must.

―――――――

Love is catholic. That which attaches itself exclusively to a single object is not love but the desire to be loved.

―――――――

The imperative "Love one another" having proven impossible, the time has come to learn how to accomplish the more modest aim of surviving one another.

The stars have no names except "sister" and "brother," and they do not use the names they have. They cannot hate because they do not love, and they cannot love because they do not hate. Nothing prevents them from burning forever.

Homo feminae lupus. Femina viro lupa.

Even when men have been dominant, neither they themselves nor women have believed them capable of dominating.

Men treat women as property because the connection between man and child is certain only if the man possesses the child's mother.

Marriage damages by its suppression of the imagination. The question "what if?" is no longer permissible.

It is astonishing that in popular culture love is valorized, when marriage is a far more interesting condition.

Love is the decision to find, and the process of finding, everything unlovable in another person.

In a world of hope, every actual event would be cause for despair. In a world of love, every action would be a death.

A child must learn to love. An adult must learn not to.

Love is the condition of being willing to believe any lie about oneself so long as it is spoken by the one individual to whom one cannot but lie and about whom one cannot but lie to oneself.

There is always an odd number of people on earth.

Love is the willingness to be damaged by liberation; liberation, the refusal to be damaged by love.

Love is possible because no joy—and no misery—is so intense that another human cannot intensify it.

The only way to get revenge on a more powerful enemy is also the only way to be faithful to the one you love: suicide.

Because love feeds on itself, it is exhausted by its own nourishment. Because hatred feeds on others, it grows stronger with its every exercise.

Silence alone is honest in the presence of one's beloved or of one's god, so only the articulate can love or worship, since even silence is meaningless when the alternative is a grunt.

To universalize the telling of lies is not self-contradictory: a community of liars would be as harmonious as a household of true lovers. We want to be lied to by others so that we will not be contradicted when we lie to ourselves.

All is fair in love and war not because there are no rules but because the rules cannot be broken.

Kings are great not because they can command service but because they can command love.

One loses solitude or gives it away before one understands its value.

All humans crave attention, but there is significant variety in the kind of attention that is the object of the craving. Some people desire the attention of one person; others, many. Some desire present attention; others, the attention of posterity. Some desire attention in the form of love; others in the form of respect.

Aging is the physiological response to the accumulated responsibilities of a life: job, spouse, friends, children, property, dying parents. An unburdened heart would beat forever.

The idea that a transcendent deity could love humans is an error of scale. The relevant analogy is not adult/child or human/dog, but human/bacterium.

A god might destroy, but would not threaten. To have to *say* you are a threat to a person is as self-negating as having to *say* you love a person.

Preparation for a descent into hell should always include the selection of a companion who is either wise or beautiful.

Postmodern Sex

Fire for the cold, words for the impotent.

That Judith can use Holofernes' own sword to castrate him and, with the same two blows, simultaneously impose on him female genitalia and penetrate them, shows the superiority of female sexuality: it contains male sexuality within it, or in other words can become male sexuality at will.

The two most exaggerated delusions a man can experience: that he is of any interest to God, and that he can experience the feelings of a woman.

Men lie because they can; women tell the truth because they must. Pregnancy is the one reality.

Bad philosophy, like bad poetry or a bad lover, tells you everything you need to know.

Western philosophy began when people started to measure genitals instead of using them.

Postmodern Virtue

Virtue is a gift of the gods. Unfortunately, there are no gods.

———————

What benefits oneself always injures another. The one human in a world of robots would be unbound by ethical obligations, incapable of doing wrong.

———————

In a world of expectation, utility is the good, and the future the source of its authority. In a world of demands, consistency is the good, and the past the source of its authority. But the present authorizes no ethic.

———————

Nihilists recognize that they cannot hope for love or wisdom.

———————

The uncompromising will eventually be compromised.

———————

Ambition and conscience are too close kin for their marriage to produce any but malformed children.

———————

One is not false for projecting a persona, nor for projecting different personae in different circumstances or to different people. One becomes false only when the circumstances or the people outside oneself dictate the choice of persona. It is no lie to be a certain way for one person and not for another—unless you *have* to be that way for that person.

A conscience, or food on the table.

The impossible always obliges.

Original sin: we have a moral obligation to know everything. We, the irremediably ignorant.

When wisdom became impossible, we sought virtue. When virtue became impossible, we sought peace. When peace became impossible, we sought health. Now that health has become impossible, there is nothing left to seek but hope, which has been impossible all along.

If every pleasure has an excess, none has a deficiency; a pleasure is always unnecessary. Therefore, the more pleasures one restricts or discards, the fewer threaten one's being good.

To build, not merely purchase or inherit, the house in which my mind will eat and walk and sleep and shit and watch sunsets and make love and wash dishes and rock in front of a fire on cold days. To hold each brick in my own hands, turn it over, look through its holes. To level the floors, plumb the walls, wire the fixtures. To know what the land was like before the house was there. To make my own hopes and plans decide what trees must be sacrificed to make way for it. To make it my own energy that raises the house, my own leaks in its roof, my own cracks in its basement floor, and my own ghost that haunts it after I am gone.

To hope only when it prompts to action, not when it substitutes for action.

Not to love life but to respect it, to be grateful to it, to do it honor.

Time engenders both hope and despair: hope because any one time will always be replaced by another, despair because any given time is always the same as any other. Similarly, time engenders both guilt and forgiveness: guilt because a moment never really leaves, forgiveness because no moment ever returns.

The times are not conducive for enacting the ideal of the "Renaissance person," but they never were. "Renaissance persons" were rare even in the Renaissance.

A mind full of birds helps only a person who can fly.

Some people inherit a personality that compels them to do one thing. Others invent a personality by doing many things.

Ignorance *is* bliss. Which makes happiness morally reprehensible.

Not deceiving others but deceiving oneself makes lying wrong.

———————

Actual-world thinkers ask why this world is as it is; possible-world thinkers ask why this world is not as it should be. To actual-world thinkers, this world proves that a god is necessary; to possible-world thinkers, this world proves that a god is impossible.

———————

Contrary to biblical teaching, hell is far harder to get into than heaven. A benevolent god would accept all who desired entry; a devil would turn away all but the best. Contrary to Aquinas's teaching, those in heaven will look down not with delight and self-satisfaction at the damned, but in a tormenting curiosity, and not because it makes their happiness complete but because they cannot look inward, having nothing there, that being the site of what could be of interest only to a devil and of use only in hell.

———————

God died not when humans stopped believing, but when they became better than God at killing.

———————

Were God moral, humans could not be.

———————

The minds of the faithful are, like their houses, open in fair weather and closed in foul.

———————

One's words, one's work, must be wiser than oneself.

———————

Only the ability to starve ourselves separates us from a swarm of flies seething above a carcass.

The flaw of rationality is that it always leads to obedience. Fortunately, even obedience can be an act of defiance.

A generous person is too timid to specify the terms of the exchange.

Greatness is achieved less by pursuit of it than by flight from the ordinary.

One courage empowers the victorious, another the defeated; one satisfaction serves the privileged, another the deprived; one wisdom restrains the powerful, another the weak.

Only from a pinnacle, where a step in any direction would be a fall, is one's shadow longer than oneself in any light.

A golden age of the spirit comparable to that of ancient Greece or Renaissance Europe is no longer possible. Leisure, the condition of such flowerings, is no longer a privilege to be exercised, but has become a problem to be solved, an emptiness to be filled. Intoxication in all its varieties has won the day.

"The windows of the soul" should be open to fresh air, but also closed to thieves.

Capitalists of the soul would be greedy and ambitious and selfish with their time and thought and energy, believing that their souls' acquisitions will not deprive and impoverish the souls of others but accrue to them.

Nobility is useless. In fact it is most visible when there is nothing to be done: after a death or in the face of one. Nobility is the alternative to despair.

The most difficult thing is not to accomplish an exacting task, but to surrender the alternative agons.

Devotees of the monotheistic religions have asked in response to the problem of evil what the world *could* be like, but not the ontologically prior question of what the world *should* be like. The real troubles of humans do not discredit a God who compensates us for those troubles, but the postulation of a God who never made troubles does.

Absurdity derives not from malevolence or indifference but from superabundance: there are too many things one ought to do, too many things one is capable of doing. Laws and taboos help restrict the ill-intentioned, but nothing helps liberate the well-intentioned.

The meaning of a word is its use; so is the meaning of an hour, and a life.

Postmodern Postscript(s)

In the preface the writer explains why he stopped where he did; in the postscript he apologizes for not having stopped where he should have.

Wisdom is not accumulated experience or accumulated knowledge, but accumulated regret.

There is a hope that calls itself faith, a hope that calls itself action, a hope that calls itself knowledge, a hope that calls itself love, even a hope that calls itself despair. And hope, like prophecy, is useless, because one cannot know which prophecies are true, which forms of hope justified until after the fact.

No future if the past cannot be erased, no past if the future cannot be forestalled.

The historian and the scientist say the past is like the future, the prophet that the past is the future.

We do not fear for the world in the face of the atomic bomb; the roaches and the algae and the tubeworms above hot springs on the ocean floor will live on. We fear for ourselves, believing that we, unlike any other life form, are indispensable. We deny about the species the same thing we deny about ourselves: that when we are gone, no one will notice, and even if we could be replaced, no one would bother to do so.

That we fear the end of the world is the one sure sign that such fear is ungrounded. The fear will be justified only when instead of fearing the end of the world, we long for it.

The objective is not, as the clichés would have it, to live in the present, but to be able to move with facility between past, present, and future, and not to wear out one's welcome in any one world.

———————

Philosophy is always autobiography, but never the autobiography it looks like.

———————

Our inability to entertain a multiplicity of ideas simultaneously and our concomitant insistence on their singularity, we call "truth."

———————

That truth confronts one directly does not imply that only truth confronts one directly. That truth confronts one directly does not imply that it confronts one only directly. That truth confronts one directly does not imply that it need not be pursued.

———————

It is difficult to tell the truth when one has to be concise, but it is also difficult under those conditions to lie.

———————

That people believe truth to be the strongest thing shows that stupidity is stronger.

———————

Not the lover of ideas but the lover of language loves truth. The noble lies of the philosopher are not noble; the noble lies of the poet are not lies.

———————

Telling the truth is not always the same as saying what one believes.

———————

The intellectual ideal is not consistency, but capacity. Not accuracy but inexhaustibility. To be able to assume a persona for whom belief in a given idea would be necessary.

A peaceful truth is an empty truth.

The passionate attempt to commit as many errors as possible would profit more than the passionate defense of a truth.

Certain fish return generation after generation to spawn at a place they have not been since birth. Certain bats can detect in perfect darkness the distance, elevation, size, speed, and direction of a moth camouflaged against a backdrop of foliage moving in a breeze. Certain pigeons can return to a specified location after having been transported hundreds of miles blindfold. Yet we talk about the revelations of our peculiar sensory apparatus as "truth."

Who can evaluate only arguments is ill-equipped to search for truth.

Length in the formulation of ideas amounts to an *ad bauculum*. Trust ideas. Distrust proof.

Delphi did not become an oracle because its prophecies were always true; its prophecies always came true because it was an oracle.

Death of the prophet: when he starts liking the sound of his own voice, and speaking from desire instead of need.

An active mind rests in the thoughts and experiences of a given text until it has gathered from that text sufficient strength to move on.

Works Cited

Albright, Daniel. 1985. *Lyricality in English Literature*. Lincoln: University of Nebraska Press.

Andreas Capellanus. 1982. *On Love*. Ed. and trans. P. G. Walsh. London: Duckworth.

Aristotle. 1941. *The Basic Works of Aristotle*. Ed. Richard McKeon. New York: Random House.

———. 1985. *Nicomachean Ethics*. Trans. Terence Irwin. Indianapolis: Hackett.

Auden, W. H. 1976. *Collected Poems*. Ed. Edward Mendelson. New York: Random House.

———. 1977. "September 1, 1939." In *The English Auden*. Ed. Edward Mendelson. London: Faber and Faber. 245-47.

Augustine. 1963. *Confessions*. Trans. Rex Warner. New York: Mentor.

———. 1984. *City of God*. Trans. Henry Bettenson. New York: Penguin.

Baker, Nicholson. 1993. *Vox*. New York: Vintage.

Barthelme, Donald. 1987. *Forty Stories*. New York: Putnam.

Barthes, Roland. 1968a. *Elements of Semiology*. Trans. Annette Lavers and Colin Smith. New York: Hill & Wang.

———. 1968b. *Writing Degree Zero*. Trans. Annette Lavers and Colin Smith. New York: Noonday.

———. 1972. *Critical Essays*. Trans. Richard Howard. Evanston: Northwestern University Press.

———. 1977. "The Death of the Author." In *Image—Music—Text*. Trans. Stephen Heath. New York: Hill & Wang. 142-48.

———. 1978. *A Lover's Discourse*. Trans. Richard Howard. New York: Hill & Wang.

Baudrillard, Jean. 1983a. *In the Shadow of the Silent Majorities*. Trans. Paul Foss, John Johnston, and Paul Patton. New York: Semiotext(e).

———. 1983b. *Simulations*. Trans. Paul Foss, Paul Patton, and Philip Beitchman. New York: Semiotext(e).

———. 1988. *The Ecstasy of Communication*. Trans. Bernard and Caroline Schutze. Ed. Sylvère Lotringer. New York: Semiotext(e).

———. 1990a. *Seduction*. Trans. Brian Singer. New York: St. Martin's.

———. 1990b. *Fatal Strategies*. Trans. Philip Beitchman and W. G. J. Niesluchowski. Ed. Jim Fleming. New York: Semiotext(e).

Bernstein, Charles. 1992. *A Poetics*. Cambridge: Harvard University Press.

Berry, Wendell. 1990. "Why I Am Not Going to Buy a Computer." In *What Are People For?* San Francisco: North Point. 170-77.

Bidart, Frank. 1983. "The War of Vaslav Nijinsky." In *The Sacrifice*. New York: Vintage. 1-30.

Blake, William. 1969. "The Marriage of Heaven and Hell." In *Complete Writings*. Ed. Geoffrey Keynes. London: Oxford University Press. 148-58.

Bloom, Allan. 1987. *The Closing of the American Mind*. New York: Simon and Schuster.

Bly, Robert. 1962. "Depression." In *Silence in the Snowy Fields*. Middletown, Conn.: Wesleyan University Press. 37.

Boccaccio, Giovanni. 1962. *The Decameron*. Trans. Richard Aldington. New York: Dell.

Brodsky, Joseph. 1986. *Less Than One*. New York: Farrar Straus Giroux.

Camus, Albert. 1972. *The Plague*. Trans. Stuart Gilbert. New York: Vintage.

Canetti, Elias. 1978. *The Human Province*. Trans. Joachim Neugroschel. New York: Farrar Straus Giroux.

Caputo, John D. 1993. *Against Ethics*. Bloomington: Indiana University Press.

Cavell, Stanley. 1979. *The Claim of Reason*. New York: Oxford University Press.

———. 1984. "The Fact of Television." In *Themes Out of School*. San Francisco: North Point. 235-68.

Cheney, Lynne V. 1989. *50 Hours: A Core Curriculum for College Students.* Washington, D. C.: National Endowment for the Humanities.

Chomsky, Noam. 1980. *Rules and Representations.* New York: Columbia University Press.

Cioran, E. M. 1991. *Anathemas and Admirations.* Trans. Richard Howard. New York: Arcade.

Coetzee, J. M. 1990. *Age of Iron.* New York: Random House.

——. 1992. *Doubling the Point: Essays and Interviews.* Ed. David Attwell. Cambridge: Harvard University Press.

Crane, Stephen. 1899. "The Trees in the Garden Rained Flowers." In *The American Tradition in Literature.* Vol. 2. Fourth Edition. Ed. Bradley, Beatty, Long, Perkins. New York: Grosset & Dunlap. 713.

Culler, Jonathan. 1975. *Structuralist Poetics: Structuralism, Linguistics, and the Study of Literature.* Ithaca: Cornell University Press.

Cutrofello, Andrew. 1994. *Discipline and Critique: Kant, Poststructuralism, and the Problem of Resistance.* Albany: SUNY Press.

Danto, Arthur C. 1981. *The Transfiguration of the Commonplace.* Cambridge: Harvard University Press.

Darwin, Charles. No date. *The Origin of Species and The Descent of Man.* New York: Modern Library.

Deleuze, Gilles, and Félix Guattari. 1983. *Anti-Oedipus: Capitalism and Schizophrenia.* Trans. Robert Hurley, Mark Seem, and Helen R. Lane. Minneapolis: University of Minnesota Press.

Deleuze, Gilles, and Félix Guattari. 1987. *A Thousand Plateaus: Capitalism and Schizophrenia.* Trans. Brian Massumi. Minneapolis: University of Minnesota Press.

Derrida, Jacques. 1976. *Of Grammatology.* Trans. Gayatri Chakravorty Spivak. Baltimore: Johns Hopkins University Press.

——. 1978. *Writing and Difference.* Trans. Alan Bass. Chicago: University of Chicago Press.

——. 1981. *Dissemination.* Trans. Barbara Johnson. Chicago: University of Chicago Press.

——. 1982. *Margins of Philosophy.* Trans. Alan Bass. Chicago: University of Chicago Press.

————. 1987. *The Truth in Painting.* Trans. Geoff Bennington and Ian McLeod. Chicago: University of Chicago Press.

Descartes, René. 1931. *Discourse on the Method.* In *The Philosophical Works of Descartes.* Vol 1. Trans. Elizabeth S. Haldane and G. R. T. Ross. Cambridge: Cambridge University Press. 79-130.

Eco, Umberto. 1986. *Travels in Hyperreality.* Trans. William Weaver. New York: Harcourt Brace Jovanovich.

Ekelund, Vilhelm. 1986. *The Second Light.* Trans. Lennart Bruce. San Francisco: North Point.

Eliot, T. S. 1970. *Collected Poems 1909-1962.* New York: Harcourt, Brace & World.

————. 1975. "Tradition and the Individual Talent." In *Selected Prose.* Ed. Frank Kermode. New York: Harcourt Brace Jovanovich and Farrar Straus Giroux.

Ellison, Ralph. 1972. *Invisible Man.* New York: Vintage.

Ellmann, Maud. 1993. *The Hunger Artists: Starving, Writing, and Imprisonment.* Cambridge: Harvard University Press.

Foucault, Michel. 1972. *The Archaeology of Knowledge.* Trans. A. M. Sheridan Smith. New York: Pantheon.

————. 1990a. *The History of Sexuality.* Trans. Robert Hurley. New York: Vintage.

————. 1990b. *The Use of Pleasure.* Trans. Robert Hurley. New York: Vintage.

Freud, Sigmund. 1950. "The Uncanny." In *Collected Papers* IV. Trans. Joan Riviere. London: Hogarth.

————. 1962. *Three Essays on the Theory of Sexuality.* Trans. James Strachey. New York: Basic.

————. 1965. *The Interpretation of Dreams.* Trans. James Strachey. New York: Avon.

————. 1977. *Introductory Lectures on Psychoanalysis.* Trans. James Strachey. New York: Norton.

Frith, Uta. 1993. "Autism." *Scientific American* 268, #6 (June): 108-14.

Frye, Northrop. 1957. *Anatomy of Criticism.* Princeton: Princeton University Press.

Gass, William. 1976. *On Being Blue*. Boston: David R. Godine.

Gates, Henry Louis, Jr. 1992. *Loose Canons: Notes on the Culture Wars*. New York: Oxford University Press.

Gilbert, Jack. 1982. *Monolithos: Poems, 1962 and 1982*. New York: Knopf.

Gleick, James. 1987. *Chaos: Making a New Science*. New York: Penguin.

Goethe, Johann Wolfgang von. 1970. *Theory of Colours*. Trans. Charles Lock Eastlake. Cambridge: MIT Press.

Gonzalez-Crussi, F. 1988. *On the Nature of Things Erotic*. San Diego: Harcourt Brace Jovanovich.

Grim, William E. 1994. "'Good-bye, Columbus': Postmodernist Satire in *Vineland*." In *The Vineland Papers*. Ed. Geoffrey Green et al. Normal, Ill.: Dalkey Archive. 154-60.

Hardon, John A. 1968. *Religions of the World*. Vol. 1. New York: Image.

Hardison, O.B., Jr. 1989. *Disappearing Through the Skylight: Culture and Technology in the Twentieth Century*. New York: Viking.

Harrison, Jim. 1982. *Selected & New Poems 1961-1981*. New York: Delta/Seymour Lawrence.

Hass, Robert. 1984. *Twentieth Century Pleasures*. New York: Ecco.

Havelock, Eric A. 1963. *Preface to Plato*. Cambridge: Harvard University Press.

Higgins, Kathleen Marie. 1991. *The Music of Our Lives*. Philadelphia: Temple University Press.

Hix, H. L. 1990. *Morte d'Author: An Autopsy*. Philadelphia: Temple University Press.

Hobbes, Thomas. 1984. *Leviathan*. Ed. C. B. Macpherson. New York: Penguin.

Huxley, Aldous. 1969. *Brave New World*. New York: Harper & Row.

Jaini, Padmanabh S. 1979. *The Jaina Path of Purification*. Berkeley: University of California Press.

Kafka, Franz. 1946. *The Basic Kafka*. New York: Washington Square Press.

————. 1961. "The Metamorphosis." In *The Metamorphosis, the Penal Colony, and Other Stories*. Trans. Willa and Edwin Muir. New York: Schocken. 67-132.

Kahn, Charles H. 1979. *The Art and Thought of Heraclitus*. Cambridge: Cambridge University Press.

Kant, Immanuel. 1951. *Critique of Judgment*. Trans. J. H. Bernard. New York: Hafner.

———. 1956. *Critique of Practical Reason*. Trans. Lewis White Beck. Indianapolis: Bobbs-Merrill.

———. 1965. *Critique of Pure Reason*. Trans. Norman Kemp Smith. New York: St. Martin's.

———. 1981. *Grounding for the Metaphysics of Morals*. Trans. James W. Ellington. Indianapolis: Hackett.

———. 1991. *The Metaphysics of Morals*. Trans. Mary Gregor. Cambridge: Cambridge University Press.

Kierkegaard, Søren. 1971. *Either/Or*. Volume 1. Trans. David F. Swenson and Lillian Marvin Swenson. Princeton: Princeton University Press.

———. 1983. *Fear and Trembling / Repetition*. Trans. Howard V. Hong and Edna G. Hong. Princeton: Princeton University Press.

———. 1988. *Stages on Life's Way*. Ed. and trans. Howard V. Hong and Edna H. Hong. Princeton: Princeton University Press.

Kosko, Bart, and Satoru Isaka. 1993. "Fuzzy Logic." *Scientific American* 269, #1 (July): 76-81.

Kristeva, Julia. 1980. *Desire in Language*. Ed. Leon S. Roudiez. Trans. Thomas Gora, Alice Jardine, and Leon S. Roudiez. New York: Columbia University Press.

———. 1987. *Tales of Love*. Trans. Leon S. Roudiez. New York: Columbia University Press.

Kübler-Ross, Elisabeth. 1970. *On Death and Dying*. New York: Macmillan.

Larkin, Philip. 1989. "Faith Healing." In *Collected Poems*. Ed. Anthony Thwaite. New York: Farrar, Straus, Giroux. 126.

Lehman, David. 1990. "The Answering Stranger." In *Operation Memory*. Princeton: Princeton University Press. 19-21.

Leiser, Burton M. 1986. *Liberty, Justice, and Morals*. 3rd Ed. New York: Macmillan.

Lévi-Strauss, Claude. 1966. *The Savage Mind*. Chicago: University of Chicago Press.

Luria, A. R. 1976. *Cognitive Development: Its Cultural and Social Foundations.* Trans. Martin Lopez-Morillas and Lynn Solotaroff. Ed. Michael Cole. Cambridge: Harvard University Press.

————. 1987. *The Mind of a Mnemonist.* Trans. Lynn Solotaroff. Cambridge: Harvard University Press.

Lyons, John. 1970. *Noam Chomsky.* New York: Viking.

Lyotard, Jean-François. 1984. *The Postmodern Condition: A Report on Knowledge.* Trans. Geoff Bennington and Brian Massumi. Minneapolis: University of Minnesota Press.

————. 1988. *The Differend: Phrases in Dispute.* Trans. Georges Van Den Abbeele. Minneapolis: University of Minnesota Press.

————. 1991. *The Inhuman.* Trans. Geoffrey Bennington and Rachel Bowlby. Stanford: Stanford University Press.

————. 1993. *Libidinal Economy.* Trans. Iain Hamilton Grant. Bloomington: Indiana University Press.

Mackey, Louis. 1986. *Points of View.* Tallahassee: Florida State University Press.

Marshall, Richard. 1988. *Robert Mapplethorpe.* New York: Whitney Museum of American Art.

Marx, Karl. 1977. *Selected Writings.* Ed. David McLellan. Oxford: Oxford University Press.

McHale, Brian. 1992. *Constructing Postmodernism.* London: Routledge.

Merwin, W. S. 1980. "Man With One Leaf in October Night." In *The Carrier of Ladders.* New York: Atheneum. 110.

Mill, John Stuart. 1979. *Utilitarianism.* Ed. George Sher. Indianapolis: Hackett.

Milosz, Czeslaw. 1983. *The Witness of Poetry.* Cambridge: Harvard University Press.

Milton, John. 1957. *Complete Poems and Major Prose.* Ed. Merritt Y. Hughes. Indianapolis: Odyssey.

Montaigne, Michel de. 1965. *The Complete Essays.* Trans. Donald M. Frame. Stanford: Stanford University Press.

Moore, Prentiss. 1981. "The Snow Leopard." In *The Garden in Winter and Other Poems.* Austin: University of Texas Press. 28.

The New English Bible. 1972. New York: Oxford University Press.

Nietzsche, Friedrich. 1968a. *The Portable Nietzsche.* Trans. Walter Kaufmann. New York: Viking.

———. 1968b. *The Will to Power.* Trans. Walter Kaufmann and R. J. Hollingdale. Ed. Walter Kaufmann. New York: Vintage.

———. 1968c. *Basic Writings of Nietzsche.* Trans. Walter Kaufmann. New York: Modern Library.

———. 1974. *The Gay Science.* Trans. Walter Kaufmann. New York: Vintage.

———. 1982. *Daybreak: Thoughts on the Prejudices of Morality.* Trans. R. J. Hollingdale. Cambridge: Cambridge University Press.

———. 1986. *Human, All Too Human.* Trans. R. J. Hollingdale. Cambridge: Cambridge University Press.

Ong, Walter J. 1982. *Orality and Literacy: The Technologizing of the Word.* London: Methuen.

Paglia, Camille. 1991. *Sexual Personae: Art and Decadence from Nefertiti to Emily Dickinson.* New York: Vintage.

Paglia, Camille, and Neil Postman. 1991. "She Wants Her TV! He Wants His Book!" *Harper's Magazine,* March. 44-55.

Peacock, Molly. 1989. "There Must Be." In *Take Heart.* New York: Vintage. 71.

Perelman, Bob. 1984. *a.k.a.* Great Barrington, Mass.: The Figures.

Plato. 1963. *Collected Dialogues.* Ed. Edith Hamilton and Huntington Cairns. Princeton: Princeton University Press.

Porchia, Antonio. 1988. *Voices.* Trans. W. S. Merwin. New York: Alfred A. Knopf.

Pound, Ezra. 1926. "The Temperaments." In *Personae.* New York: New Directions. 100.

———. 1968. "The Serious Artist." In *Literary Essays of Ezra Pound.* Ed. T. S. Eliot. New York: New Directions. 41-57.

Pynchon, Thomas. 1990. *Vineland.* Boston: Little, Brown.

Rawls, John. 1971. *A Theory of Justice.* Cambridge: Harvard University Press.

Santayana, George. 1962. "The Cognitive Claims of Memory." In *Philosophy in the Twentieth Century*. Vol. 1. Ed. William Barrett and Henry D. Aiken. New York: Random House. 425-33.

Sartre, Jean-Paul. 1963. *Saint Genet: Actor & Martyr*. Trans. Bernard Frechtman. New York: Pantheon.

Saussure, Ferdinand de. 1966. *Course in General Linguistics*. Ed. Charles Bally and Albert Sechehaye. Trans. Wade Baskin. New York: McGraw-Hill.

Schlegel, Friedrich. 1991. *Philosophical Fragments*. Trans. Peter Firchow. Minneapolis: University of Minnesota Press.

Shakespeare, William. 1980. *Complete Works*. 3rd ed. Ed. David Bevington. Glenview, Ill.: Scott, Foresman.

Singer, Peter. 1990. *Animal Liberation*. New York: Avon.

Skinner, B. F. 1972. *Beyond Freedom and Dignity*. New York: Bantam.

Spivak, Gayatri Chakravorty. 1976. "Translator's Preface." In Derrida, *Of Grammatology*. ix-xc.

Stevens, Wallace. 1942. *The Necessary Angel*. New York: Vintage.

———. 1982. *Collected Poems*. New York: Vintage.

Stevenson, Mrs. Sinclair. 1984. *The Heart of Jainism*. New Delhi: Munshiram Manoharlal.

Swift, Jonathan. 1729. "A Modest Proposal." In *The Norton Anthology of English Literature*. Vol 1. 4th Edition. New York: Norton. 2144-51.

Tagg, John. 1992. *Grounds of Dispute: Art History, Cultural Politics and the Discursive Field*. Minneapolis: University of Minnesota Press.

Tennyson, Alfred. 1974. "The Charge of the Light Brigade." In *The Poetical Works of Tennyson*. Boston: Houghton Mifflin. 226-27.

Tolstoy, Leo. 1960. *Anna Karenina*. Trans. Joel Carmichael. New York: Bantam.

Wheelwright, Philip. 1960. *The Presocratics*. Indianapolis: Bobbs-Merrill.

Whitman, Walt. 1975. "Song of Myself." In *The Complete Poems*. Ed. Francis Murphy. New York: Penguin.

Wilbur, Richard. 1963. "Epistemology." In *The Poems of Richard Wilbur*. New York: Harcourt Brace Jovanovich.

Wittgenstein, Ludwig. 1958a. *Philosophical Investigations.* 3rd edition. Trans. G. E. M. Anscombe. New York: Macmillan.

———. 1958b. *The Blue and Brown Books.* New York: Harper and Row.

———. 1961. *Tractatus Logico-Philosophicus.* Trans. D. F. Pears and B. F. McGuinness. London: Routledge & Kegan Paul.

———. 1967. *Zettel.* Ed. G. E. M. Anscombe and G. H. von Wright. Trans. G. E. M. Anscombe. Berkeley: University of California Press.

———. 1972. *On Certainty.* Ed. G. E. M. Anscombe and G. H. von Wright. Trans. Denis Paul and G. E. M. Anscombe. New York: Harper.

———. 1974. *Tractatus Logico-Philosophicus.* Trans. D. F. Pears and B. F. McGuinness. London: Routledge & Kegan Paul.

———. 1978. *Remarks on Colour.* Ed. G. E. M. Anscombe. Trans. Linda L. McAlister and Margaret Schättle. Berkeley: University of California Press.

———. 1980. *Culture and Value.* Ed. G. H. von Wright with Heikki Nyman. Trans. Peter Winch. Chicago: University of Chicago Press.

———. No date. *Lectures and Conversations on Aesthetics, Psychology and Religious Belief.* Ed. Cyril Barrett. Berkeley: University of California Press.

Worton, Michael, and Judith Still, eds. 1990. *Intertextuality.* New York: Manchester University Press.

Yeats, William Butler. 1969. *Mythologies.* New York: Collier.

Zukofsky, Louis. 1981. "Poetry." In *Prepositions: The Collected Critical Essays.* Berkeley: University of California Press. 3-11.

Zwicky, Jan. 1993. *Lyric Philosophy.* Toronto: University of Toronto Press.

Index of Names